Praise for *You Are Worth It*

"My opening three words for every speech made to some one-million audience members is, 'You are worthwhile.' Now, Louise Griffith takes that thought and weaves a magical guide to 52 weeks of underlining that fact by declaring 'You Are Worth It.' Her life experiences and deep soul forge a gift for every reader. You do indeed deserve to know that you are equipped to see yourself in every mirror of life and declare to that image, 'you are worth it.' Louise's book will guide you to that declaration."

—**Bob Danzig**, Former President, Hearst Magazine
Enterprises, Author of *The Leader Within You*, and
Inductee of The Speaker Hall of Fame

"Louise has a rare gift in offering a simple, yet powerful process in this book that will carry you back home to honoring, nurturing, and loving who you truly are in this world."

—**Molly Harvey**, author, *Outstanding Leadership*, speaker,
visionary leader and CEO of Molly Harvey Global, UK

"This book is a must-read for anyone who has questioned, 'Am I worth it?' Louise will guide you in reaffirming your worth regardless of your circumstances."

—**Christine Clifford**, CSP, award-winning author, *Not Now...
I'm Having A No Hair Day, The Clue Phone's Ringing...It's
for You! Healing Humor for Women Divorcing*, speaker,
president and CEO, The Cancer Club® and Divorcing Divas®

"*You Are Worth It* touches the heart and ignites the soul to remind each of us that we are indeed worth it. No one will believe it if we do not. Each word, each sentence, each chapter speaks authentically to create a catalyst of change for good. Spectacular book and one you will refer to each and every day!"

—**Julie Gilbert Newrai**, CEO & Founder, Precioustatus, former senior vice president, Enterprise Innovation and Growth, Best Buy, Co.

"Are you tired of all the demands and expectations life throws at you? If so, you're in the right place. This book will nourish your soul. Louise takes you on a beautiful journey of self-discovery so that you can step fully into the person you were created to be."

—**Deirdre Van Nest,** Professional Speaker and creator of the Speak and Get Results Blueprint, www.speakandgetresults.com

"Louise lights the way by asking the questions that will help you overcome the limiting beliefs that stop you. I encourage you to take the fifty-two week journey to realize you are worth it!"

—**Judy Kay Mausolf**, Author of T*A-DAH! Get Happy in 5 Seconds or Less*, Speaker, Coach and CEO of Practice Solutions, Inc.

YOU ARE WORTH IT

52 Weeks to Honoring, Loving,
and Nurturing Your Soul

LOUISE GRIFFITH

ISBN 13: 978-1-940014-32-6
eISBN 13: 978-1-940014-35-7

Library of Congress Catalog Number: 2014948348
Printed in the United States of America
Third Printing: 2017
21 20 19 18 17   7 6 5 4 3

Cover design by Nupoor Gordon
Interior design by Gabe Levine

Wise Ink Creative Publishing
Minneapolis, MN
www.wiseinkpub.com

To order, visit www.itascabooks.com or call 1-800-901-3480.
Reseller discounts available.

This book is dedicated to five
of the most precious children I know:

Jake, Michaela, Lucas, Madeline,
and Jack.

I am blessed to be your Nana.

You are bright shining lights in the world.

May you always know you are worth it.

YOU ARE WORTH IT

52 *Weeks to Honoring, Loving, and Nurturing Your Soul*

FOREWORD
By Mark LeBlanc

Are you worth it?

Yes, you are. And if you doubt that for even a moment, then you are right where you need to be. In your hands, you hold a special book. Louise will not only guide you on your journey; she will shine a light on who you are, and help you reveal who you were always meant to be.

In a world that puts too much emphasis on perfection, Louise leads us on a path of awareness and self-discovery. And, in the end we understand just how perfect we are, even with our imperfections. It will take a commitment to read, reflect, and write the answers that come from your head and your heart. It will take courage to examine your actions, activities, and events from your past that may have dimmed the light on your possibilities.

I met Louise years ago. Her spirit, filled with a deep sense of compassion and authenticity, is rare indeed. She has traveled her own journey of ups and downs while helping others with her expertise in human training, coaching, and counseling. She is the real deal when it comes to exploration of what makes each of us tick in our own unique way, and inspiring people to action in the direction of their dream.

Read her book, hear her speak, and if you have the opportunity to work with her, you will never be the same. Her ability to help you see yourself in a new light will unlock a combination of truth and acceptance. It will help you embrace your potential for the next chapter of your life and work. As you embark on your 52-week journey, you will slowly feel your spirit come alive, and soon the momentum you feel will be unstoppable. At times, it will be uncomfortable, and that is okay. Because you have this book in your hands, you must be seeking change, and now change is possible for you.

Louise is one shining light in this world, and if there were a parade in your honor, she would be the best one to lead the way. Take one week at a time and move forward with knowing you can always take just one more step, no matter what you are facing or how you are feeling.

Louise and I are both cheering you on!

—Mark LeBlanc, speaker, coach, pilgrim, author of
Growing Your Business and *Never Be the Same*

INTRODUCTION

The lotus flower grows in muddy and murky water, far away from the sun. It slowly rises above the surface to bloom with remarkable beauty, without even a drop of mud on it. During the night, the lotus closes and sinks under the water, emerging again with the sunlight of a new day. It blooms in spite of unfavorable conditions.

The lotus flower represents life. Just as the lotus flower grows up from the mud into an object of great beauty, people also grow and change, and become more beautiful. The lotus flower can represent a hard time in life you have overcome. The sunlight reminds us of the hope of a new day. As the lotus begins to emerge, we are encouraged never to quit when things seem difficult. The blossom of a lotus flower embodies enlightenment, our awareness, and beauty.

So this is your time to bloom, to come out of the mud now holding you fast to old ways. Rise in your own beauty to each day's inviting sun.

You are worth it. You truly are. Imagine a big beautiful door with the word "IT" sketched across in gigantic gold lettering. You've seen this door for a long time, and have been tempted to open it. However, every time you go to open this special door, something stops you. You can't do it. You can't open this door. If we were honest, we'd admit we frequently have these doors in our lives, which can be painfully difficult to ignore, though somehow we find ways to avoid "it." We pretend "it" doesn't exist. Or worse, we convince ourselves we're happy without "it." To take it a step further, the most common reason many of us don't open those "doors" is because we don't believe we are worth the goodness waiting for us on the other side of "it."

You are a being designed to bring about purpose, joy, and fulfillment, not only to others, but to yourself. Whether it's a healthier lifestyle, a new adventure, or cutting ties to a person in your life who no longer deserves your energy, we convince ourselves we're "fine" with things as they are.

For years, I lived that way. I believed "fine" was good enough, even though in my coaching business, I encourage my clients to strive for pure and soul-thriving joy. It wasn't until one day, on a nature walk surrounded by beautiful flowers and lush trees, I noticed how at peace the birds were as they chirped and flew all around me. I felt the warmth of the sun on my face, and breathed in the clean, fresh air. As joy surged through me, I whispered, "Louise, you deserve to be this happy. Fine is *no longer good enough*. You are worth 'it.' "

Each of us has gone through (or may now be going through) losses, challenges, heartaches, and transitions in life, which can be painful and discouraging. Hopefully, we grow through our experiences and difficulties, learning lessons along the way, and we are then able to be present to ourselves and to others in a meaningful and life-giving way. Like a lotus flower, our life is a process of unfolding and becoming.

Several years ago, while exercising at Curves, a young woman to my left, told me she had recently lost sixty-five pounds. Being curious, I asked what made her decide to lose weight at this time in her life. Her answer: "I woke one morning, and I just decided I was worth it."

Her words, *"I decided I was worth it,"* simply wouldn't leave my being. It haunted me in a good way. It seemed she had just given me a "golden nugget" for life. If we do not think we are worth it, whatever our "it" is, "it" may not ever happen, or not as soon as it could, or to the extent it can.

As I pause and reflect, it seems for years I have asked myself some variation of the question, "Am I good enough?" Research confirms that among the majority of people, this basic question is prevalent. This is also consistent with the work I have done with individuals in my role as a psychologist and success coach. The impact on our lives can lead to a downward mental and emotional spiral of feelings of unworthiness. Self-confidence and self-esteem are challenged. This is often triggered by a false mental image of perfection, which as we know is unattainable. We miss out on opportunities available to us. The very good news is that we get to challenge and change those beliefs, therefore, experiencing different outcomes.

Writing this book is a small triumph, illustrating how remarkable we can be when we follow our spirits, and trust we are more than good enough for something great. It has been within my soul since the day I was born.

So, what's behind your "it" door? What's waiting for you on the other side? Even more, what keeps you from opening this beautiful door? I hope by Week 52, you'll be confident in your purpose, and serene in your spirit as you confront the barriers now holding you back. And then I hope you proudly follow your soul as it guides you to the abundant life you are meant to live.

You are worth it!

WEEK 1

Embrace "I Am *More Than* Good Enough"

If I could give you one key, and one key only to a more abundant life, I would give you a sense of your own worth, an unshakable sense of your own dignity as one grounded in the source of the cosmic dance, as one who plays a unique part in the unfolding of the story of the world ....

—Greta Cosby

- How would your life change if you believed you were good enough?
- How would it feel to embrace the fact you are indeed *more* than good enough—and you have inside of you all you need to live life fully, with confidence, while making valuable contributions to others?

You may ponder how this could be true. Go ahead.
It is a great concept to explore.

If you're worried that embracing the idea you're more than good enough is the same as being arrogant, think again. Owning your gifts and talents with the intention of living more fully, joyfully, and peacefully, isn't the same as having an inflated ego. In fact, when you accept the fact you are more than good enough, you'll begin to help others see they are also good enough. Loving yourself is a light illuminating and nourishing not only your spirit—but the spirits of others, too. Embrace the idea you have the power to decide you are good enough. No one can take your power away from you. You own the key to your self-worth, which governs all you do.

In order to achieve the feeling of being good enough, you have to believe it first. As the author of your own life script, you can choose how you want to think and believe.

> *Loving yourself is a light illuminating and nourishing not only your spirit— but the spirits of others, too.*

I Am Worth It Next Steps:

1. Make the choice this week to intentionally have life-giving thoughts and beliefs about yourself. Examples: I am a fantastic friend, mother, and wife. I deserve a promotion for the hard work I have done. I'm beautiful inside and out, and I need to change nothing in order to love myself more.

2. Reflect on the opportunities and dreams you will pursue as you believe and know you are more than good enough. What is possible for you?

3. How will you present yourself in both familiar and new situations involving other people?
4. Journal about how these insights move you toward being whom you REALLY are and reclaiming your "it" at this time in your life.

Examples for Week 1 to help you focus:

Based upon my observations and insights this Week:

I will stop *giving away my personal power to others.*

I will start *focusing on the positive things I do, instead of the negative things*.

I will continue *believing there is always hope.*

Now YOU fill in the blanks below.

Based upon my observations and insights this week:

I will stop _____

_____.

I will start _____

_____.

I will continue _____

_____.

You will know your next step because you are wise, and you can reclaim your true essence now.

You ARE Worth It!

WEEK 2

Illuminate Your Own Possibilities

We must be willing to get rid of the life we've planned, so as to have the life that is waiting for us.

—Joseph Campbell

Making plans is both exciting and motivating. They point you in directions you want and need to go. View them as a map showing you all the possible destinations your life can embark upon. You certainly can't predict bumps, detours, or the storms you may encounter along the way. Do not focus on things that could go wrong. Instead, create broader outlines allowing for flexibility and resiliency.

As you are in the midst of carrying out your plans, remember to be curious and open to the lessons you may learn along the way—lessons you didn't intend or expect to happen. These are some of life's sweetest and often undervalued gifts. "What if?" may become two of your most favorite words. They can expand your horizon significantly. You will perhaps meet amazing new people. You may be exposed to opportunities which otherwise might never have appeared in your life had it not been for the "detour."

"Possibility thinking" is a learned skill. When practiced often, it can become a lifelong habit and a way of life. Go ahead. Try it on. Notice your energy level as you do.

Be curious and open to the lessons you may learn along the way—lessons you didn't intend or expect to happen.

I Am Worth It Next Steps:

1. List the ways your plans have stopped you from experiencing all life has to offer.

2. How comfortable are you moving forward, honoring your intuition, without knowing specific details?

3. Is your filter of life positive or negative? What do you focus on first?

4. Reflect on a time in your life when something did not work out as planned, and yet the results were much better than you had planned.

Based upon my observations and insights this week:

I will stop _____

_____.

I will start _____

_____.

I will continue _____

_____.

You are wise and are open to unlimited possibilities upon which you can take action immediately.

You ARE Worth It!

WEEK 3

Choose Your Story

Loving ourselves through the process of owning our story is the bravest thing we'll ever do.

—Brené Brown

We often see life through our own perspective, based on interpretations of our own experiences and life events. You might be tempted to visit an old or even false reality. Don't go there anymore. When you speak as though an old or false reality is still true, you step backwards. By continuing to tell your old story, you recreate the person who holds you there.

Hard things happen. Life is not fair. People are not always kind. We each have our own agenda and are on our own soul's path. Don't allow people and circumstances to make you disorganized inside. When we do this, we're unable to move forward.

Think back to a time you've watched children play with Legos, especially a Legos kit where the picture and instructions were all there. The finished product was constructed according to the instructions. However, at some point, it gets disassembled. In the end, the perfect Lego structure becomes individual pieces spread all over the floor. Although it may seem like a disaster to see your hard work undone—no longer the creation you intended—the good news is another structure can be built using those same pieces.

Every story has a reframe when we look at it from a different perspective and in light of the lessons learned. You are the *only one* who can make it happen. It takes a while, and it often requires some internal healing to move from the old story to the new story. It is possible, and you are the one to make it happen, often with the help of others.

> ***If your story isn't making you feel worth it,
> choose a new one.***

I Am Worth It Next Steps:

1. What payoff do you receive by telling your old story in which you struggled, and were perhaps hurt by another person or by life's circumstances?
2. Reflect and journal about what is getting in your way of releasing your story. Next, create a new story containing some of the same components with an entirely different focus and perspective.
3. Who can help you change your story?
4. Which story makes you feel more worthy and honoring of you without blaming anyone else?
5. What is a new story you want to create in your life, which you have not yet experienced?

Based upon my observations and insights this week:

I will stop _____

_____.

I will start _____

_____.

I will continue _____

_____.

You are wise, and you will know which story to choose.
The process does take time and some work on your part.

You ARE Worth It!

WEEK 4

Have Honest Conversations with Yourself

If you do not ask yourself what it is you know, you will go on listening to others, and change will not come because you will not hear your own truth.

—Saint Bartholomew

Avoidance, another form of fear, may have you focus on everything but the reality of your life right now. If you have awakened from your self-imposed trance of denial, you may have to make changes in your life for which you do not feel prepared.

What do you know absolutely to be true for you? How scary is it for you to go to a spot of knowing? Until now, you may not have thought you were good enough or worth it, and so it seemed it was a waste of your time and energy to think about it.

Spending quiet time reflecting and journaling about it allows you to know your truth. Knowing it, whatever your "it" may be, doesn't mean you have to take action on it immediately. It can help you to stay grounded to yourself and to your truth, which can also inform your choices and actions as you move forward.

What if others around you wouldn't agree with you or support you? Perhaps you will choose to not speak up right at that moment in this specific situation. However, it doesn't mean you need to abandon your own truth. Make your own set of rules to live by instead of conforming to someone else's. Hopefully, you have a trusted friend with whom you can share your thoughts. If you don't at this particular moment, look around and trust your intuition as you test the waters to find someone. You can be there for each other.

> *Avoidance, another form of fear, may have you focus on everything but the reality of your life right now.*

I Am Worth It Next Steps:

1. How often do you let the opinions of others impact how you think, feel, and act?

2. Do you feel you have the right to have your own truth and opinions?

3. What would you discover if you had an honest conversation with yourself?

4. Reflect upon a time you knew your truth and acted upon it, or at least moved toward it.

Based upon my observations and insights this week:

I will stop _____

_____.

I will start _____

_____.

I will continue _____

_____.

You are wise and will come to initiate and honor these conversations more frequently.

You ARE Worth It!

WEEK 5

Identify Your Internal Script

The most influential and frequent voice you hear is your inner voice. It can work in your favor or against you, depending on what you listen to and act upon.

—Maddy Malhotra

Many of you learned to surrender your wisdom and intuition early in life. Do you remember hearing any of these messages as a child?

- Be nice.
- Be quiet.
- Be good.
- Do what I tell you.
- Be seen and not heard.
- Don't get too excited.
- Don't be too bright.
- Don't toot your own horn.
- Don't get a big head.
- Be happy with what you have.

- Don't rock the boat.
- Who do you think you are?

The list can go on and on. These statements made sense to the adults saying them. Perhaps they hoped to motivate you in some way. However, these statements were about them and their journey. You were young and might have believed the statements at face value. Only you know which negative messages you still hold on to as part of your internal dialogue.

Imagine what your life might have been like if, as a child, you had been given these messages, which became your truth:

- Be proud of who you are and what you know.
- Trust you will know what to do next.
- You have important things to say.
- You are smart.
- You are courageous.
- Think big.
- Follow your dreams.
- You are wise.
- You count.

These are messages you can tell yourself today and every day, as well as the children with whom you interact. The good news (or the bad news, depending on how you choose to see it) is that you continue to be the author of your internal script. You are the only one who can "cut, paste, and delete" messages no longer serving you or others.

The thoughts you think have the most positive influence over your life. Train yourself to listen to your wisdom rather than your limiting thoughts and beliefs. You, and only you, sit at the table as the head of the board of your mind.

> *Only you know which negative messages you still hold on to as part of your internal dialogue.*

I Am Worth It Next Steps:
1. Which of these messages is still part of your current dialogue or current story?
2. Which messages became rules you lived by?
3. How have these messages and beliefs influenced and impacted your life today?
4. Specifically, which messages and thoughts can support your "willingness to be worth it?"
5. How dare you? How dare you not?

Based upon my observations and insights this week:

I will stop _____

_____.

I will start _____

_____.

I will continue _____

_____.

You are wise and the author of your internal script.

You ARE Worth It!

WEEK 6

Be Open to Change

That's the risk you take if you change: that people you've been involved with won't like the new you. But other people who do will come along.

—Lisa Alther

What comes to your mind as you see, hear, or think about the word "change?" Perhaps you get excited. Or do you tense up and feel hesitant and scared? It is possible you have a fear of the unknown and would rather stay in "status quo" mode until it finally becomes unbearable.

As you decide and *know* you are worth it, whatever your "it" may be, there are likely to be major and minor shifts in relationships, some positive and some negative. People are used to counting on you to be one way, the way you have always been or have always shown up as being. I have experienced such reactions. It's as though certain people and groups of friends do not know what to "do" with the new YOU. Looking at the world through their eyes makes sense. It may not even be judgmental on their part. The pattern and relationship as they know it is different and unfamiliar to them. They may not know how to interact and respond.

In order to make a change in life, you need to have a defined clear vision of what you want to accomplish, as well as the choices available to you. Be specific.

A change of scenery and your environment can also bring a change in perspective. As you go through this week, be curious about changes you can create and experience. Be open to the transformation change can and will bring in your life.

> **Be open and curious about changes you can create and experience.**

I Am Worth It Next Steps:

1. In what areas of your life have you made the most change?
2. What areas of your life do you want to change?
3. What outcome do you envision when you make these changes, and how would your life be different?
4. How would these changes serve you and others?

Based upon my observations and insights this week:

I will stop _____

_____.

I will start _____

_____.

I will continue _____

_____.

You are wise and will know what changes are right for you at this time in your life.

You ARE Worth It!

WEEK 7

Know Your Core Values

In matters of style, swim with the current; in matters of principle, stand like a rock.

—Thomas Jefferson

Your own set of values determines which aspects of life you regard as important or beneficial. Maybe your values are spiritually oriented. Perhaps you're a vegetarian or someone who prides yourself on being environmentally conscious. Whatever your values are, they influence your tastes and your way of life, as well as your interactions with others. Your values may evolve and shift through the years as you grow and mature and experience different stages in your life.

Your own unique set of core values is at the foundation of your life and impacts your choices. Your personal core values are the attributes motivating and guiding you in your life through the decisions and choices you make. Many people lead lives disconnected from their core values—those beliefs most important to them. As a result, they may experience unhappiness, discontent, and lack of fulfillment. Conflict may appear and create an internal dissonance.

Sometimes individuals support other people's values, often ignoring their own. It is important for you to identify your core values and what really matters most to you. It is a significant source of personal power. When you honor those values, you can know your self-worth because you are congruent and authentic. You can also discern the ways in which you and your life need to change in order to incorporate your values.

> *Whatever your values are, they influence your tastes, your way of life, as well as your interactions with others.*

I Am Worth It Next Steps:

1. What is most important to you in your life?
2. What is a core value of yours that others may not know?
3. How do your life, work, and relationships at this moment help fulfill your personal values?
4. What one change will you make to be more congruent with your core values?

Based upon my observations and insights this week:

I will stop _____

_____.

I will start _____

_____.

I will continue _____

_____.

Stay true to your core values. They are important and help to define who you are.

You ARE Worth It!

WEEK 8

Honor Your Wisdom

If you don't honor your own soul, who will?

—Louise Griffith

What happens when you don't follow your inner guidance and wisdom? Have you noticed a "gentle nudge" inside you regarding whether or not to go in a certain direction? Think about the moments when you paid attention to your intuition, as well as the times you ignored it? What was the outcome?

It has been said wisdom is to the soul what health is to the body. Wisdom brings perspective to help inform your choices. Know at the core of your being what is right for you, even if others don't understand. Remember, you can *always* change your mind.

You may know that the old way of thinking and being is no longer working for you, and now you have no choice but to embrace the unknown. Trust yourself, and trust that you will be guided. Your perceptions are often more accurate than you acknowledge. Wisdom is blocked by the intensity of fear, anger, and panic and leaves you feeling disconnected from yourself and your truth. A wisdom-based decision is never dictated by fear. Pause and check inside yourself to see how you are feeling. Breathe deeply. Get grounded. Stay grounded. You will know the next step for you.

> *Know at the core of your being what is right for you, even if others don't understand.*

I Am Worth It Next Steps:

1. What do you know is your truth at this time in your life?
2. What if the timing is not right for you?
3. How will you know when it is?
4. Who can help you gain more clarity?
5. Reflect upon the many times you have honored and followed your inner wisdom, often called intuition, which has had a profound impact in your life?

Based upon my observations and insights this week:

I will stop _____

_____.

I will start _____

_____.

I will continue _____

_____.

You are wise, and you can trust your inner voice as you pause and listen—really listen.

You ARE Worth It!

WEEK 9

Reclaim Your Personal Power

When I dare to be powerful—to use my strength in the service of my vision—then it becomes less and less important whether I am afraid.

—Audre Lorde

Personal power is your ability to change the direction of your life. It is the energy fueling your actions. It is not about "power over" another human being, but the power coming from within yourself. Personal power allows you to focus your attention in the area of your choice.

Perhaps you learned to surrender your personal power early in life as you worked hard to please others and live up to their expectations. You may have been taught in subtle and not-so-subtle ways to live by rules imposed upon you. As time went on, you may not have realized you did indeed have choices.

Once you make a choice and decide you are worth it, no matter what your "it" is at this moment in your life, you become the decision maker and are in the driver's seat of your life. You have the power to choose, which no one can take away from you. Personal power is about being in alignment with your thoughts, feelings, integrity, and soul. You are the one *who can* make it happen. Personal power is based on strength, confidence, and competence you acquire as you move toward self-realization. With a little imagination and a lot of determination, you can make miracles happen.

> *Personal power is about being in alignment with your thoughts, feelings, integrity, and soul.*

I Am Worth It Next Steps:

1. When you hear the term "personal power," what does it bring up for you?
2. In order to claim your full power, what do you choose to leave behind?
3. What do you need to do so you can live in the moment and not be reacting to the past?
4. What do you choose to step into—something over which you *do* have control?
5. Name three of your greatest assets ready to support you right now. Focus on these this week.

Based upon my observations and insights this week:

I will stop _____

_____.

I will start _____

_____.

I will continue _____

_____.

**You are wise and can reclaim your internal personal power.
The time is now.**

You ARE Worth It!

WEEK 10

Make Conscious Choices

If you limit your choices only to what seems possible or reasonable, you disconnect yourself from what you truly want, and all that is left is compromise.

—Robert Fritz

A conscious choice is one you make in full cognition of reality without being influenced by pressure from the outside or from within. Choices define who you are and who you become. A choice is a choice only when you know you have one. Some people prefer to think they don't have any choices, so they can blame others and are not accountable for their actions or the part they contributed to a situation.

You can let your thoughts be in control and spend a lifetime reacting to the consequences, or you can choose to be in control of your thoughts and actions. In order to do so, you must be conscious and live in the moment, knowing *only you* can make the choice before you.

You can't change the circumstances of a situation; however, you can change your reaction to it. Align your decisions with what matters most to you. A choice *based in fear* seals in the belief you are unworthy or not good enough and strong enough to be in control of your own life, thoughts, beliefs, and choices.

You won't always know if a decision is a good or bad one until you commit to a choice. Undoing the choice may be painful, and yet it can be done. As in all of life, there are lessons one can learn at these pivotal moments.

> *Be conscious and live in the moment,*
> *knowing only you can make the choice before you.*

I Am Worth It Next Steps:
1. What benefits are available to you and to others when you choose to respond rather than react?
2. Is there a choice you had made you now regret and would do differently if given the opportunity again?
3. What, however, did you learn from having made a certain choice?
4. What is one choice you have made in your life of which you are extremely proud?

Based upon my observations and insights this week:

I will stop _____

_____.

I will start_____

_____.

I will continue _____

_____.

You are wise and can learn from every choice you make.

You ARE Worth It!

WEEK 11

Cultivate Your Resilience

In the depth of winter, I finally learned that within me there lay an invincible summer.

—Albert Camus

Resilience is the process of adapting well in the face of adversity, trauma, tragedy, threats, or significant sources of stress. These may include family and relationship problems, serious health problems, or workplace and financial stressors. It is the ability needed to find the inner strength for you to bounce back from a setback or a challenge.

Being resilient doesn't mean going through life without experiencing stress and pain. Emotional pain, sadness, anxiety, and fear are common in people who have suffered major adversity or trauma in their lives. Resilience is the internal capacity to adapt successfully in the face of threats or disaster.

Resilience is a trait that can be learned and developed. Resilience develops as we age and gain better thinking and self-management skills. Rely on the caring and supportive relationships in your life because they will be the most help to you. Accept help from people who care about you and who will listen to you. Explore resources available to you, such as support organizations within your community. Churches often have excellent support groups where everyone is welcome. Many of my clients over the years have benefited greatly from participating in various groups. You can also explore online resources.

Increase your resilience as you:

- Maintain a positive view of yourself.
- Have confidence in your strengths and ability to solve problems.
- Look for opportunities for self-discovery.
- Keep things in perspective.
- Maintain a hopeful outlook.
- Visualize what you want rather than what you fear.
- Take action.
- See yourself as resilient rather than as a victim.
- Take excellent care of yourself!

> *Resilience is the internal capacity to adapt successfully in the face of threats or disaster.*

I Am Worth It Next Steps:

1. Think back to two times in your life when you encountered difficult challenges and rose above them.

2. What were some of your inner resources that helped you be resilient?

3. What did you learn about yourself and your interaction with others in the process?

4. Is there someone in your life right now who would benefit from some extra care from you?

Based upon my observations and insights this week:

I will stop _____

_____.

I will start _____

_____.

I will continue _____

_____.

You are strong and have what it takes to move through challenging situations.

You ARE Worth It!

WEEK 12

Nourish Your Spirit

A bird doesn't sing because it has an answer; it sings because it has a song.

—Maya Angelou

What ignites the flame inside you? What inspires you? The best reason to do anything is simply because you enjoy doing it. The joy is in the action, not the result. Therefore do not attach a goal to it. Be in the moment and connect with the joy inside of you. Whatever you choose is a part of your "song."

If you love to dance, dance. If you love to sing, sing. If you love to read, read. If you love to cook, cook. If you love gardening, be in the garden. If you love to meditate, meditate. If you love to do yoga, do yoga. If you like certain types of exercise make sure you do them. If you love music, surround yourself with the music you enjoy. If you appreciate art, make sure you are near it often, even surrounded by it. If you love to act, find a way to express yourself. If you enjoy being with certain people, set up a time to get together. If you appreciate solitude, make sure you create time for it. Create your own sacred space and be there often. Be curious, add new experiences, and cherish your favorite activities which nourish and soothe your soul.

Nature has a magnificence all of its own. It provides transformation through the various seasons and the vast array of different types of beauty—be it a sunrise, sunset, mountain, plain, forest, ocean, a lake, river, and even a pond. It helps to restore inner peace, tranquility, and clarity of mind. Immerse yourself in nature and be there often. It's important you discover and know what your "song" is and sing it often.

> *The best reason to do anything is simply because you enjoy doing it.*

I Am Worth It Next Steps:
1. What are you tolerating that no longer serves your higher good?
2. What top three things nourish your spirit?
3. How often do you experience these? If not often enough, what do you let get in the way?
4. What one new thing will you add to your life to stretch yourself?

Based upon my observations and insights this week:

I will stop _____

_____.

I will start _____

_____.

I will continue _____

_____.

You are wise, and your spirit knows what is nourishing for you.

You ARE Worth It!

WEEK 13

Trust Yourself

Trust yourself. Create the kind of self that you will be happy to live with all your life. Make the most of yourself by fanning the tiny inner sparks of possibility into flames of achievement.

—Golda Meir

You have to have faith and trust in others; however, if you do not trust in yourself, you are lost. Trust yourself to be, to do, and to have the best in life. Trust yourself to create the reality you want to have.

Part of trusting yourself is realizing you will make mistakes from time to time. *If you are not making mistakes, you are not learning anything new*. Perhaps you are stuck in a rut. See your mistakes and failures as gifts, which are valuable learning tools. Often you learn the most from the things you do wrong, knowing you will have an opportunity to do them differently in the future. Catch yourself doing things right, and make a mental note while encouraging yourself.

Avoid the "blame game" whereby you become a victim who is helpless and cannot change your fate. In doing so, your mistakes and failures are attributed to external circumstances.

Take responsibility for your choices and actions. Forgive yourself more often, letting go of the anger you hold against yourself and others. These are two important foundation pieces for building trust within oneself.

Concentrate on following your intuition. It takes courage and faith in yourself to follow where your heart and inner guidance lead, especially when the rational mind suggests you should not. By doing so, you strengthen the trust you have in yourself, allowing you to rely on your own strengths and abilities. Celebrate your accomplishments. Try something new. Whenever you begin something new, you are starting afresh with a clean slate. As you put some effort into your new venture, notice your energy level and sense of well-being. Cheer yourself on. You can trust you have everything inside of you to create the life you desire.

> *Catch yourself doing things right,*
> *and make a mental note while encouraging yourself.*

I Am Worth It Next Steps:

1. What valuable lifelong lesson have you learned from a recent mistake?

2. Think of times when acceptance from others took a higher priority over trusting yourself. What was the outcome?

3. Would you rather be responsible and accountable for

your choices and actions, or would you rather blame someone else?

4. What are some situations in your life where you can absolutely trust yourself?

Based upon my observations and insights this week:

I will stop _____

_____.

I will start _____

_____.

I will continue _____

_____.

You can trust yourself because you are wise, authentic, and open to learning.

You ARE Worth It!

WEEK 14

Pause Often

There comes a time when the world gets quiet and the only thing left is your own heart. So you'd better learn the sound of it. Otherwise you'll never understand what it's saying.

—Sarah Dessen

In your busy, over-scheduled life, you often forget to intentionally rest, breathe, and pause. It is so easy to get lost in busyness and to live life in automatic-pilot mode. To-do lists, inboxes, and non-stop demands can run your day. You may not slow down because of the fear of not getting enough done. For many of you, the demands of your lives weigh you down as work, home, and family incessantly compete for your attention.

When you find your mind becoming cluttered, pause and take a breather. Watch the wind blow through the trees, take a moment to smell the fresh air outside, and look around you to observe the beauty surrounding you. *Breathe!* Pausing helps you regain control of your thoughts and emotions. It also helps you avoid miscommunication. When you pause, you create space to consider a different perspective or a more effective response to the challenges in your life.

Many of my coaching clients have come to appreciate the power of a pause, especially in pivotal moments throughout the day. Pausing allows them to be at the head of the table of their own mental advisory board and to stay in the driver's seat of their lives. As a result of making the conscious choice to pause, they experience more freedom, control, confidence, and clarity. You may not be able to change the events occurring in your life; however, you can change your reaction to them.

> *Pausing helps you regain control of your thoughts and emotions.*

I Am Worth It Next Steps:

1. Are you currently living on high alert? What price do you pay for this frantic way of living life?
2. Reflect upon a recent situation in which pausing before reacting might have been a better choice.
3. When experiencing strong emotions such as anger, pause to see what triggered within you.
4. How will you remind yourself to pause this week?

Based upon my observations and insights this week:

I will stop _____

_____.

I will start _____

_____.

I will continue _____

_____.

Many options open up for you as you choose to pause more often.

You ARE Worth It!

WEEK 15

Set Realistic Expectations

When no one around you seems to measure up, it's time to check your yardstick.

—Bill Lemley

An expectation is a belief that something should happen in a particular way, or someone or something should have a specific quality or behavior. "Realistic" means something is based on the facts and situations as they really are. As you well know, life is unpredictable. When you set goals and make plans, a big part of you expects, or for sure hopes, those things will happen. However, changes and surprises are inevitable. You have a choice when these surprises occur. You can see them as a source of frustration, or you can see them as part of the adventure of living—a consequence of being alive.

It has been said that expectations are "premeditated resentment" if they are unrealistic. When the reality of a situation appears and is not in alignment with your "expectations," you might experience anxiety, depression, stress, anger, fear, and a multitude of other emotions.

Understanding and dealing with the difference between

"realistic" and "unrealistic" has profound implications, both personally and professionally. A few thought patterns can contribute to this experience. The most familiar are: "Take on too much," and "Make sure you do it perfectly."

Unrealistic expectations as to how everyone and everything should function can cause great stress and conflict in relationships.

Unrealistic expectations about what you can actually accomplish in a given amount of time and in the situation you are currently experiencing, can at the moment invite you to "pause" and ask yourself if this is indeed realistic or unrealistic. Looking at the world through another's eyes will give you a magnificent perspective.

> *Unrealistic expectations can cause great stress and conflict in relationships.*

I Am Worth It Next Steps:

1. Which of your expectations for yourself, and for others, may not be realistic?
2. What is the impact on you and on the others?
3. Reflect upon the difference between setting goals and having an expectation as to the outcome.
4. When have you had high expectations for yourself that served you well? When have you fallen short, and what was the impact? Has this ever led to your feelings of not being "good enough?"

5. What if you hurt or disappoint others by saying, "no," or you decide to not live up to their expectations for you?

Based upon my observations and insights this week:

I will stop _____

_____.

I will start _____

_____.

I will continue _____

_____.

You are wise and will take the time to figure out the balance required in this arena.

You ARE Worth It!

WEEK 16

Shift Your Perspective

I murmured because I had no shoes until I met a man who had no feet.

—Persian Proverb

When you are in the midst of a problem, it is easy to lose perspective because you are too close to it. As you pause and consider your situation from a different perspective, you'll see there is always hope, and you can triumph over tragedy. Look at the bigger picture, and identify the real problem. You may find it is smaller than you think.

The dark times in your life feel like they last much longer than the happy times, which may skew your perspective. Remember the wisdom of the seasons: spring always follows winter. Your "winter" won't last forever. Keep your eyes on spring. Darkness, like sorrow, doesn't last forever. Just as dawn follows night, joy follows sorrow.

Being able to shift your perspective is a very powerful tool that's available in your resource bag. Picture a kaleidoscope. As you first look into it, you see one pattern. As you turn it ever so slightly to the right or the left, a different pattern appears. You are the one choosing to make the shift.

As you become conscious of negative thinking or judgment about a person or situation, shift your perspective, knowing you can create a different outcome by thinking different thoughts.

When you choose to see every circumstance in your life as an opportunity to evolve and grow, you will always have options. The ability to look at the world through another's eyes helps you see new ways of viewing people and situations. Make the conscious choice to approach each perspective with an open mind.

> *In the kaleidoscope of life, you are the one choosing to make the shift.*

I Am Worth It Next Steps:

1. Think of a time when you viewed a situation from a different perspective. What did you notice? What was the outcome?

2. What current situation you are viewing negatively? Would you be open to viewing it from a different perspective? If so, try it now. What did you experience?

3. As you reflect upon something that currently seems like a problem, focus on concrete steps you can take to resolve it.

4. What are two conscious shifts in your thinking you will make this week?

Based upon my observations and insights this week:

I will stop _____

_____.

I will start _____

_____.

I will continue _____

_____.

**You are wise and will pause to consider different perspectives
as you move forward.**

You ARE Worth It!

WEEK 17

Rise Above Resignation

It's a funny thing about life; if you accept anything but the best, you very often get it.

—Somerset Maugham

Some people have the attitude that something unpleasant must happen—and they cannot change it. You may hear them say, "It is what it is." Unpleasant things do happen and cannot be changed, such as losing a job, ending a relationship, or permanently losing something of value. Sometimes people use this phrase to rationalize their own disappointment. It is usually better to recognize reality and to move on, rather than to stay in a perpetual state of anger and despair over what has occurred.

The phrase "it is what it is" can also be a formula for settling, when in reality, something better is possible. Individuals may become resigned to the "status quo" of their lives, believing there are no other options. They often settle for less and make do. Can you sense the discouragement and often despair accompanying this thought process? This way of thinking can also become a habit.

The good news is so much more is often possible. Stay open to new options. Look at life and current situations from a new perspective. Remember the strengths and gifts you bring to life. Remember times in your life when something seemed hopeless, and yet, you made it work. You figured out a solution, often with the help of others. This *can happen* again and again and again.

> **Don't become resigned to the "status quo" of your life, *believing you have no other options.***

I Am Worth It Next Steps:

1. As you reflect on your life, can you think of a time when you chose to settle for less? What was the outcome? What did you learn from this experience?

2. Also, remember a time when you made something work in spite of the challenging circumstances involved. What was the outcome? What did you learn from this experience?

3. Which of your internal resources did you use to make this happen?

4. What is your next challenge?

Based upon my observations and insights this week:

I will stop _____

_____.

I will start _____

_____.

I will continue _____

_____.

When you know you are worth it, you will not settle for less in life.

You ARE Worth It!

WEEK 18

Acknowledge and Overcome Your Fears

*The defense force inside us wants us to be cautious, to stay away
from anything as intense as a new kind of action. Its job is to
protect us, and it categorically avoids anything resembling danger.
But often it's wrong.*

—Barbara Sher

Fear, described as "false evidence appearing real," can
have a powerful impact on your decision to "be worth
it, "whatever your "it" may be. Fear is the most powerful
negative tool the mind has.

Fear drowns out the voice of wisdom. It is a self-induced
prison keeping you from really living fully. If you live your
life on autopilot, you don't have to grow, change, self-correct,
forgive, or be vulnerable. Fear gives you permission to remain
closed when your spirit yearns to be free and open. Every time
you make a choice based in fear, you are sealing in this belief: you are unworthy, and you are not good enough or strong
enough to be in control of your life, thoughts, beliefs, choices,
and future. Every time you make a choice based on fear, you
teach your mind to believe you are helpless, hopeless, and
powerless. As a result, you may feel like a victim.

Remember your worst fears aren't facts, nor are they the catastrophe your mind has conjured up in a futile attempt to protect you. It is impossible to avoid everything that scares you. If you let them, fears can hold you back from experiencing the fullness of life. Keep your mind engaged and your spirit courageous. The best cure for an irrational fear is to face it straight on while sticking to your original plan. The panic of fear can blow things out of proportion. You know wise things. Face your fear and talk yourself through it. Faith, which gives you hope and can help you see options and possibilities, can be eroded by fear.

Your fears are also clues about hidden issues inside of you that invite healing. Think about it.

- What fear keeps you from addressing, moving past, and conquering?
- What would your life be like if your fears weren't holding you back?
- What would you do if someone told you today you no longer had to worry about the thing of which you're most afraid?

Fear of the unknown can have a huge grip on you. What if the "unknown" was actually a huge blessing to you in your life? It is possible. Are you open to this possibility?

> *If you let them, fears can hold you back*
> *from experiencing the fullness of life.*

I Am Worth It Next Steps:

1. How has fear kept you from doing the things you long to do?

2. What if, from your perspective, your choice to move forward seems to add more negative consequences?

3. Do you remember seeing the truth, ignoring it and/ or being afraid of it? How did you compensate or overcompensate for it?

4. How have you allowed fear to prevent you from making changes you really want to make in your life?

5. When have you let fear interfere with standing up for yourself?

Based upon my observations and insights this week:

I will stop _____

_____.

I will start _____

_____.

I will continue _____

_____.

You are wise and strong, and you can take action in the face of fear.

You ARE Worth It!

WEEK 19

Abandon Shame

Shame is the intensely painful feeling that we are unworthy of love and belonging.

—Brené Brown

Shame cuts you off from all that is real. Shame is a learned emotion, and when reinforced and internalized, you no longer feel shame—*you are shame*.

The difference between shame and guilt is evident when one makes a mistake. Shame focuses on the self. Your internal dialogue might be "I am bad. I am a loser. I am a mistake." Guilt focuses on the behavior. Your internal dialogue may be "I did something bad. I am going to say I am sorry. I made a mistake."

When you experience shame, you feel badly about yourself. You may disapprove of your own actions or accomplishment and therefore feel inferior as a human being. You do not feel you are worthy of joy, happiness, success, and the good things life has to offer. You may hide, not owning and sharing the incredible gifts and strengths you have inside of you. If you dwell on your shortcomings, you can get distracted from taking constructive action. This can lead to a cycle of self-destructive behavior.

Help and healing are possible. Become aware when something or someone triggers your shame. Notice what you experience physically and emotionally. Check in with your thinking at the moment. Are your thoughts supporting your success, or do they sabotage your efforts at moving forward toward your goals and dreams? Instead of viewing your thoughts as absolute truths, see them as mental events to observe and evaluate. Be willing to challenge shame-based thoughts and replace them with more accurate thoughts.

Excellent resources are available on the Internet, as well as in books on this subject. You may also want to seek the help of a professional to journey with you through this process of abandoning shame. You are so worth the investment you make in yourself and in your healing.

If you dwell on your shortcomings, you can get distracted from taking constructive action.

I Am Worth It Next Steps:
1. What do you tell yourself when you make a mistake?
2. How have you let shame hold you back from pursuing your dreams and honoring your soul's purpose?
3. Name three of your positive qualities that make a

contribution to others and to the world around you. Focus on these this week.

4. Is something bothering you and building up within you, making you feel bad? Connect with a person who you know cares about you, whom you trust, and who is a good listener. Doing so can give you great comfort and support. You do not need to journey alone.

Based upon my observations and insights this week:

I will stop _____

_____.

I will start _____

_____.

I will continue _____

_____.

You have great worth and value as a human being. Honor and celebrate that.

You ARE Worth It!

WEEK 20

Stop Comparing Yourself to Others

Be yourself; everyone else is already taken.

—Oscar Wilde

As you reflect upon this topic this week, think of the times or situations when you have compared yourself to others. What has been the outcome? As you pursue your passion, you have discovered there are others who are both "better" than you and others who are less accomplished in specific areas. You need to throw yourself wholeheartedly into the experience and find joy in it. Comparing yourself to others is not the least bit productive. Be who you are.

A coaching client of mine, who is an executive director of an organization, felt intimidated going into board meetings because she saw the other board members as being the real "experts" in their fields. Because of their impressive titles and accolades, she saw herself as "less than." I reminded her of her strengths, gifts, and accomplishments. I also challenged her to own the precious and unique qualities she brought to the board table. As she reflected upon these qualities, as well as the experience she brought to these meetings, she agreed to change her way of thinking and establish a new behavior of walking into those meetings with her head held high. While she was comparing herself to the others in the room, the others were likely interested in hearing her thoughts and ideas about the issues at hand. After several discussions, she experienced more confidence at future meetings and found herself speaking up and sharing her opinions, knowing her contributions were equally valuable to everyone else's.

> *Comparing yourself to others is not the least bit productive.*

I Am Worth It Next Steps:

1. What are some of the ways you have compared yourself to others? What was the impact on your self-worth?
2. Compare yourself to yourself. What are you doing today you *could not* have done one, three or five years ago?
3. In what ways have you grown that brings you joy and satisfaction? Hold on to your essence.
4. Focus on your strengths with gratitude and think of ways you can make contributions to others.

Based upon my observations and insights this week:

I will stop _____

_____.

I will start _____

_____.

I will continue _____

_____.

**I choose to show up in the world being whom I am and know
I make a difference.**

You ARE Worth It!

WEEK 21

Surrender Your Regrets

The bitterest tears shed over graves are for words left unsaid and deeds left undone.

—Harriet Beecher Stowe

Regretting is a waste of precious time and energy.

The "if only" syndrome can consume your creative energy and create tunnel vision. "If only I'd … ," "If only I hadn't … ," "If only they … ," "If only I had known." These statements come from a sense of discouragement combined with fear, ignorance of the possibilities in life, and fear of taking risks within those possibilities.

Regrets can keep you stuck in the past unless you resolve to do something different and make a different choice the next time the opportunity arises. Regrets are different from guilt because guilt can be about good intentions one never had in the first place. If you say you feel guilty, it somehow exonerates you above the choice or deed. Regrets imply when experiencing the same situation again in the future, you will make a different choice. Experiences like this inform you to new possibilities in thinking and actions. Some examples are:

"I will never dishonor myself again;" "I choose to be all I am;" "I choose to live life fully;" "I choose to pause and mindfully proceed."

Life is precious. Relationships are precious. You are precious. What do you know is the next step you need to take in certain relationships or situations? What is holding you back from taking action?

> **_Regretting is a waste of precious time and energy._**

I Am Worth It Next Steps:
1. What is your greatest regret in life?
2. What is the greatest lesson you learned from that experience?
3. What will you do differently next time?
4. For what have you forgiven yourself?
5. For what have you not forgiven yourself?

Based upon my observations and insights this week:

I will stop _____

_____.

I will start _____

_____.

I will continue _____

_____.

You will learn from the past and make wise choices now and in the future.

You ARE Worth It!

WEEK 22

Assume Personal Responsibility

Take your life in your own hands and what happens? A terrible thing: no one to blame.

—Erica Jong

When you decide to take your life in your own hands, new energy and possibilities open up. When you ask yourself, "What's my part?" you give yourself the power and permission to move through the situation rather than being bogged down, trying to get others to change. You become proactive rather than reactive or defensive. You quit making excuses.

You have a sense of how to make different choices in the future in order to produce a different outcome. You will feel you are in charge of your life, and no one has power over you. When you choose to be accountable, there is nothing more to say. The next step is moving forward, asking forgiveness if you violated or hurt another person in the process. It is honoring your right to create a life for yourself that is fulfilling and alive.

It can hurt to accept responsibility for your actions and choices; however, it can also be very liberating and empowering. Blaming others may seem like a safe and comfortable option, which can also keep you in a trance and in denial. It can also drain your energy and life source because at a deeper level you know it is not true.

A freedom, as well as increased peace and joy, comes with being accountable. You don't need to blame anyone. You want to use your precious energy to learn the lessons available to you and move forward with courage and conviction.

> *Quit making excuses—be responsible.*

I Am Worth It Next Steps

1. Do you have a resistance to being accountable?
2. Were there times in your life when you were overly responsible?
3. Which is more natural for you—to blame someone else or to assume personal responsibility? Was it always this way?
4. Think of a time when you assumed personal responsibility for a situation that you see you helped create. What was the impact and how did you feel?

Based upon my observations and insights this week:

I will stop _____

_____.

I will start _____

_____.

I will continue _____

_____.

You are wise and continue to grow in this area while experiencing more joy and freedom.

You ARE Worth It!

WEEK 23

Evaluate Your Self-Care

Wellness means acknowledging the resilience of the human spirit. It means being at peace with oneself; it means finding a balance between self-care and reaching out to others.

—Ruth Stricker

Think of depositing money into a bank. In doing so, you can make withdrawals when needed. And so it is with self-care. The bank can be thought of as your soul. Become a student of good nutrition so your body is fueled properly. A poor diet can make you more vulnerable to stress. There are so many options for exercising. Do what you enjoy, and stretch yourself to experience something new. See it as an adventure. Frequent exercise is an imperative part of your self-care program. It can be great for you physically and mentally. Exercise provides a stress release and keeps your body healthy. Look at your options, make choices, and schedule them into your busy life. If you do what you like or take on the challenge of learning new things, it can also *be fun*.

Protect your mind and treat it well. How many hours of TV do you watch? What kind of programs do you choose to watch? What types of movies do you watch? If you love to learn, what have you done to expand your learning? What classes have you taken? What kind of books do you read?

Be kind to yourself. Love yourself for all of the good you see, and accept your flaws and the fact you are imperfect. Make a choice to stop self-criticism. Acknowledge your effort, and let go of worry. Trust yourself. You do know more than you think you know. Forgive yourself if you have made mistakes in the past causing you to feel less worthy.

If you want to be in charge of your life, monitor these areas because they do impact your life, energy, and often the relationships you have with yourself and others. This is an area over which you do have control.

> *Love yourself for all of the good you see,*
> *and accept your flaws and the fact you are imperfect.*

I Am Worth It Next Steps:

1. What do you know is life-giving to your self-care at this moment?
2. How often are you making this happen?
3. What are you letting get in the way?
4. Commit to one specific thing or practice you will do every day this week to contribute to your self-care in a positive way.

Based upon my observations and insights this week:

I will stop _____

_____.

I will start _____

_____.

I will continue _____

_____.

You may begin to love yourself more deeply beginning now. It is your best first step to excellent self-care.

You ARE Worth It!

WEEK 24

Grow in Gratitude

If the only prayer you say in your whole life is "Thank you," that would suffice.

—Meister Eckhart

Gratitude is defined as a felt sense of wonder, thankfulness, and appreciation for life. It is more than simply a pleasant emotion to experience or a polite sentiment to express. It can be a basic disposition that seems to make lives happier, healthier, more fulfilling, and even longer, as supported by psychological research:

- The practice of gratitude as a spiritual discipline may cure excessive materialism and accompanying negative emotions of envy, regret, resentment, disappointment, bitterness, and other psychological states harmful to long-term happiness.
- Grateful people experience higher levels of positive emotions—happiness, vitality, optimism, and hope—and greater satisfaction with life.
- Grateful people appear to be more socially oriented. They are more empathic, forgiving, helpful, and supportive than their less-grateful counterparts.

When you express genuine gratitude for things both large and small, you shift into a positive space where you experience the joy that comes from appreciating all you already have. It is easy to forget and take those things for granted. Gratitude is a positive magnet that attracts more of the things you want in life. The price is also right. It is a habit you can form beginning today. Remember: you are the one who chooses your thoughts.

A spiritual practice for many is, before getting out of bed, to think of three to five things for which they are grateful. It is an excellent way to start the day. You can also write these things in a "gratitude journal" of your own creation or one of many available for purchase. It can be very interesting to look back over the weeks, months, and years, and re-read your entries.

> *Gratitude is a positive magnet that attracts more of the things you want in life.*

I Am Worth It Next Steps:
1. What three things are you truly and deeply grateful for at this time in your life?
2. Of the 86,000 seconds available to you each day, how many seconds do you spend saying, "Thank you?"
3. Reflect on your life to-date. Who is one person who is still alive who had a powerful, positive influence in your life? Communicate your gratitude and appreciation to that person this week.

4. As you reflect upon your strengths and gifts, which three are you most grateful for this week?

Based upon my observations and insights this week:

I will stop _____

_____.

I will start _____

_____.

I will continue _____

_____.

You can cultivate this habit of expressing gratitude for your benefit and also for the benefit of others.

You ARE Worth It!

WEEK 25

Choose Your Attitude

Change the things you can; change your attitude about the things you can't.

—Maya Angelou

Your attitude can be based on the weather, the amount of traffic congestion, the way people treat you, or a number of other external factors—or your attitude can be exactly what you choose for it to be. When you turn your attitude over to other people or circumstances, it can be volatile, undependable, and not very productive. When you choose your own attitude, independent of what is happening around you, you set yourself up to make positive progress and to be more in charge of your life.

An attitude is a point of view about a situation, a lens through which you see life. It is made up of three parts: what you think, what you do, and what you feel. Regardless of what situation you are in, you always have certain thoughts about it. You also have an emotional response to it, and you behave a certain way in it. To begin changing your attitude, change the way you think, act, or feel. It is easier to change your thoughts or behavior than to change your emotions. Usually your emotions get your attention in a situation. You may not like experiencing sadness, anger, anxiety, or frustration, and you may do your best to have those emotions change. Sometimes, however, being *angry* or *sad* is what is called for in a situation. Be aware of what your attitude is, and know it does affect you and others. Once you are aware of the impact, you may view your attitude differently, even if the person or situation hasn't changed. You will be more successful by going back to changing your thinking or behavior because those are two areas over which you have more control.

It is best when that lens is focused on positive possibilities. Your attitude can enable you to make the most of challenging situations and also find and create enormous value in the world. There is nothing that forces you to adopt one particular attitude over another. Get in the habit of consciously choosing a positive, empowering attitude. You then become free to achieve the things most meaningful to you. In addition, you can choose the impact you want to have before entering a difficult situation.

Once you accept that you are the *only one* who is choosing your attitude at this moment, you can decide whether to keep it or shape it into an attitude that is more life-giving both to you and to others.

> *Get in the habit of consciously choosing a positive, empowering attitude.*

I Am Worth It Next Steps:

1. Do you believe that whatever your attitude is at the moment, it is one you are choosing? Reflect upon the implications of this being true.

2. Does your attitude help or hinder you and others? Is it helping you be the way you want to be?

3. Are you able to switch your attitude when the one you have chosen is not working?

4. What are specific things you can do to remind yourself of the attitude you want to demonstrate every day? What are the benefits of this choice?

Based upon my observations and insights this week:

I will stop _____

_____.

I will start _____

_____.

I will continue _____

_____.

You are the only one who can choose and control your attitude. How awesome is that?

You ARE Worth It!

WEEK 26

Be Courageous

Courage is fear that has said its prayers.

—Dorothy Bernard

Courage is a state of "being," rather than "doing." It is to be held close, developed, and savored. Your inner courage will direct you to the areas of your life calling out to be changed. The rewards of honoring this are far greater than the risks, even though you certainly may not have a sense of the outcome. When you stand in courage, you make powerful choices for yourself.

Find the courage to be who you really are. It is within you, and no one can take it away from you. Courage is the willingness to act, even when frightened. Give yourself permission. You have the right to be different from how others think you should be. Identify your wants, needs, and feelings. Be yourself. Find the courage to live the life you love and live it powerfully.

Courage is the key to conquering your objectives. Without it, you would not take the first step or take necessary risks to achieve your dreams and goals. Confidence, courage, and a spirit of sacrifice are essential to get you to where you really want to go. Courage engages your heart.

You are the expert on doing something to take you out of your comfort zone. It is not about "right or wrong." It is not about comparing comfort zones. It is about honoring your truth with a sense of adventure and fun. What is courageous for you is to live your absolute truth. Honor that.

Without courage, all other virtues would be obsolete and fail to exist. It takes courage to display passion, humility, honorability, integrity, truth, confidence, strength, compassion, and vulnerability on a day-to-day basis. It is also the foundation piece of the essence of who you truly are.

> *Courage engages your heart.*

I Am Worth It Next Steps:

1. As you reflect over your life, do you see when you first began to lose courage?
2. How did you regain it?
3. What are three courageous things you have said or done of which you are very proud?
4. Where do you find the courage to make the changes you know you need to make in spite of the reactions of others? It is there.

Based upon my observations and insights this week:

I will stop _____

_____.

I will start _____

_____.

I will continue _____

_____.

You have the wisdom and courage to take your next step. You know what it is.

You ARE Worth It!

WEEK 27

Ask Yourself: Am I Pleasing Others at My Expense?

You can't please everyone. When you're too focused on living up to other people's standards, you aren't spending enough time raising your own. Some people may whisper, complain, and judge. But for the most part, it's all in your head. People care less about your actions than you think.

—Kris Carr

This week, ask yourself:

- How often have you pleased others rather than being true and authentic?
- Have you ever gone along with the crowd to avoid being the only one left standing on the outside?

It's natural to want to be liked. Pleasing others to fit in is important at various stages in our lives. Respect that!

However, there is a difference between choosing kindness, respect, and compassion, and denying your true wants and needs. When you please others in the hope of being accepted, you subtly lose your self-worth in the process. You waste valuable time and energy on things beyond your control.

Don't fall into the trap of becoming addicted to the recognition of putting others' needs first. It can become a full-time career. This gives a false sense of increased self-worth. The "recognition trap" reinforces a people-pleasing mindset, which leads to your needs becoming less obvious and important. Remember, being of service to others does not mean sacrificing yourself.

Most people want to belong, fit in, and be liked by others. You can do so while honoring your own wants and needs as you pay attention to others. It does not need to be an "either/or" proposition. As you move forward, pause and ask yourself the question: is always pleasing others before yourself really working for you?

You can please others—and still take care of yourself.

I Am Worth It Next Steps:

1. Write down a memory of when you first learned it would benefit you to please others and put their needs first.

2. Think about an instance when you tried to please someone, and then found yourself resenting the person you were trying to please. What was it all about?

3. Decide on three nice things to do for yourself this week just because you are worth it.

4. Pick one person whom you trust to hold you accountable, who will call it to your attention when you're pleasing others before choosing your own health and happiness.

Based upon my observations and insights this week:

I will stop _____

_____.

I will start _____

_____.

I will continue _____

_____.

You will know because you are wise and can make choices that honor you as well as others.

You ARE Worth It!

WEEK 28

Set Clear Boundaries

Don't compromise yourself. You are all you got!

—Janis Joplin

Do you ever find yourself saying, "But they need me. If I don't do it, who will?" The truth of the matter is others may "need" your gifts, time, and even financial support because you have much to contribute. Your willingness to help can make others' lives easier and perhaps less stressful. The important thing is whether or not their request will work for you. How often do you say "Yes," when your internal wisdom is telling you to say "No?" Listen to your inner voice because it wants to protect you from spreading yourself too thin. Be clear. You might say something like, "Thank you for thinking of me. At this time, I am going to say 'No.'" You really do not have to explain why. It is your right to do so.

Saying "No" can be one of the most honoring things you can do for yourself. When you set a boundary, you might disappoint the person making the request. It's okay. Boundaries are not always comfortable to establish; however, they're a bridge to receiving the peace and freedom you deserve. They help keep you from becoming overstretched and resentful in the long run. Speak up, and ask for what you want. It is also your birthright. Remember, you teach others how to treat you. Setting boundaries is part of any caring relationship. Negotiating to get your own needs met helps you know and trust yourself, and it also helps others know and trust you as well.

If your limits are violated, speak up. Allowing people to take advantage of you isn't noble or necessary, especially when you can do something to stop it.

> **Remember, you teach others how to treat you.**

I Am Worth It Next Steps:

1. Pay attention. Do you tolerate the intolerable? Do you normalize the abnormal? Do you accept the unacceptable?
2. What price have you paid for these choices?
3. Can you forgive yourself for the times you let it happen?
4. Do you know what it feels like to be treated with respect and dignity from others and also from yourself? Reflect and take note of the impact.
5. Reflect upon a time when you set very clear boundaries with another person. Regardless of the outcome, as you go deep within, how did you feel?

Based upon my observations and insights this week:

I will stop _____

_____.

I will start _____

_____.

I will continue _____

_____.

You will know because you are wise, and you have the wisdom and courage inside of you to set clear boundaries.

You ARE Worth It!

WEEK 29

Guard Your Safety

A ship is safe in harbor, but that's not what ships are for.

—William Shedd

Many women have given up the true courageous warrior inside them in exchange for approval from others, for position, and for the illusion of safety. The price one pays is difficult to calculate because potential and possibilities are often not explored.

Fear will have you choose what you believe will keep you safe, even when the opposite is true. It will have you believe that you can't do it, the cost is too high, the path ahead is too difficult—and you are wrong. It will encourage you to stay where you are, and know it is not the right time to deal with whatever you are considering. Inertia may set in. In spite of the fact you do not know the details of the future, your intuition is still telling you the time is now; however, you may not want to move forward.

On the other hand, there are times and situations in which you may not feel safe physically or emotionally. If so, it is essential to set clear boundaries. It may be necessary for you to say, "Stop. No more." If your request isn't honored, you may have to leave your situation either temporarily or permanently. It is not okay for someone to violate you in any way. Reach out for help. You do not have to journey alone.

> *Feeling a need for safety could cause you to stay where you are.*

I Am Worth It Next Steps:

1. When have you settled for less in order to feel safe? What was the outcome?
2. What have you gained by setting clear boundaries with others?
3. Is there any area of your life in which you are continuously making compromises?
4. Take a risk this week that would honor you and be out of the ordinary for you.

Based upon my observations and insights this week:

I will stop _____

_____.

I will start _____

_____.

I will continue _____

_____.

You have the right to feel safe in all areas of your life.

You ARE Worth It!

WEEK 30

Pay Attention to the People You Allow in Your Life

Surround yourself with the dreamers and the doers, the believers and things, but most of all, surround yourself with those who see the greatness within you, even when you don't see it yourself.

—Edmund Lee

It is important to surround yourself with supportive, heart-centered people who make you feel safe and secure and give you positive energy. It is also important to identify people in your life who drain your energy and belittle you, often making you feel unworthy. Dr. Judith Orloff, MD, refers to this type of person as an "emotional vampire." Dr. Verna Cornelia Price, Ph.D, has brilliantly referred to this type of person as a "subtractor" or a "divider."

Being around such people can catch you off guard because it can be a subtle process. The result can be chronic anxiety or depression of varying degrees. You may not speak out because you don't want to be seen as "difficult" or uncaring. It is possible you have been led to believe it is your fault, and you are to blame.

Beware of passive-aggressive people. They may not seem angry on the surface; however, they act in the same way as those who are completely carried away by their rage. Guard yourself against them. When people express their displeasure overtly, feelings move through them quickly. When emotions are bottled up, they last a long time.

It is unacceptable for the mean-spirited to violate you. Take a stand against people who drain you of your inner light. It is an excellent form of self-care, and it leads to more joy, peace, and freedom. Let go of those who bring you down, and surround yourself with those who believe in you and bring out the best in you.

Filter out critics. When you believe in yourself, the opinions of others don't matter. Don't waste time listening to why you can't do something. Surround yourself with "can-do" people, not naysayers. Maintain a "can-do" spirit. Enlist cheerleaders, people who know the real you. When you falter, they can restore your faith by sharing their strong belief in you. Fill your calendar with the people who lift you up and who believe in you.

Surround yourself with people who make you feel safe and secure and give you positive energy.

I Am Worth It Next Steps:

1. Who adds to and invigorates your energy?
2. Who in your life is draining your energy at the moment?
3. Do you see yourself as having a choice between feeling tortured and victimized, or feeling liberated?
4. What life lessons can you learn from this experience?
5. What are your next steps?

Based upon my observations and insights this week:

I will stop _____

_____.

I will start _____

_____.

I will continue _____

_____.

You deserve to be with people who love you and who believe in you and your dreams.

You ARE Worth It!

WEEK 31

Nurture Healthy Friendships

If I had a flower for every time I thought of you ... I could walk through my garden forever.

—Alfred Tennyson

Great friendships are priceless. Good friends can lift your spirits, make you laugh, and remind you that you are loved. Friends make you feel comfortable with yourself. You do not need to act like someone you are not. You know each other's shortcomings and love each other anyway.

Healthy friendships are based on mutual respect, trust, and support. Each person is valued for who she is and what she brings to the relationship. Differences in thoughts, feelings, and values are accepted and respected. You listen to one another in a non-judgmental manner and value each other's opinions. You put effort into attempting to understand and affirm the other person's emotions. You support each other's goals in life, wanting the very best for each other.

You communicate openly and honestly, admitting mistakes or being wrong. Your friend will not lie to you, nor will she try to hurt your feelings. You know where you stand with your friend and will not be afraid to share your true opinions and feelings. As a result, healthy friendships will not let underlying tension or negativity linger very long. They address issues, forgive, and move on. Doing so can reduce stress and disease.

Great friends will nurture your relationship and still encourage you to meet people and try new things on your own. You are excited for the adventures you create together and those you experience with others. You call forth the best from each other because you care deeply about one another. Connecting with your friends is actually good for your health.

Let your friends know how much you appreciate them by thanking them for supporting you. Make a quick call to say, "I could not have done it without you," or, "Thank you for the time you took to listen. It means a great deal to me."

> *Great friends will nurture your relationship and still encourage you to meet people and try new things on your own.*

I Am Worth It Next Steps:

1. Who makes your heart smile, even giggle, at certain times?

2. Which of your relationships are balanced in terms of giving and receiving?

3. What is your personal definition of a healthy relationship?
4. What are some of the gifts and strengths you bring to relationships?
5. Which friend will you reach out to this week? When and how?

Based upon my observations and insights this week:

I will stop _____

_____.

I will start _____

_____.

I will continue _____

_____.

You are a pure gift to others because of who you are as a person.

You ARE Worth It!

WEEK 32

Be Vulnerable

Vulnerability is the birthplace of innovation, creativity, and change.
—Brené Brown

Choosing to be vulnerable with those in your life with whom you have an intimate relationship can be scary, if you view vulnerability as a weakness. When you share deep parts of yourself, you run the risk of being judged by others. This often happens when you are not being authentic. There is the possibility you will be misunderstood, labeled, or, even, rejected. You may then feel a sense of shame, which is easily understood as "the fear of disconnection," as researched by Brené Brown. Beneath this is the thought process, "I am not good enough" (thin enough, wise enough, smart enough). You fill in the blanks. The vulnerability you try to avoid may be the very key to successful relationships.

You may also miss out on a deep, rewarding experience, which is joyful, fulfilling, and liberating.

Your nervous system is built so you are alarmed by the more vulnerable emotions. When feelings such as disappointment, sadness, fear, and powerlessness are evoked, your alarm bells go off. You often react in a way to restore a more pleasant equilibrium. You may get busy trying to change the circumstances, pushing to get your way, hoping to avoid the feelings of fear or disappointment that are alarming you. Or you may start a campaign of numbing out—going to the refrigerator, watching TV, shopping, or pouring yourself a stiff drink. You have your own unique history of avoiding vulnerable feelings.

However, true happiness lies deep down in your vulnerability, where your desire and capacity for intimacy sleeps, and where qualities such as kindness, compassion, and sweetness are sourced. Your joy can only be as deep as your capacity to feel sadness. The depth of your compassion is directly proportional to your ability to feel hurt and rejection. Satisfaction in life depends on your ability to feel disappointed when things don't go as you hoped and planned.

Vulnerability is so much easier when you love yourself, including the less stellar parts. When you love all of you, you won't worry so much if someone else doesn't. When you are less afraid of rejection, you step into that right place of openness. Vulnerability takes practice. You will still have moments where you are more guarded and less willing to share the real you. Life will continue to give you opportunities to consciously choose openness. The rewards of vulnerability are immeasurable. You experience true connection—true love for yourself and others. You also experience a sense of worthiness, love, and belonging. You let go of who you thought you needed to be in order to be who you are.

Dare to be vulnerable to tell the story of who you are with your whole heart. Have the courage to be sincere, honest, and open. This opens the door to deeper communication all around. You will draw the people to you who will truly connect with you on a deeper level because they know exactly who you are. They like all of it and all of you, including your imperfections. They see your depth and your wisdom.

> *When you love all of you, you won't worry so much if someone else doesn't.*

I Am Worth It Next Steps:

1. Take twenty minutes this week to watch Brenè Brown's TEDxHouston presentation on "The Power of Vulnerability," filmed in June of 2010.

2. With whom will you share some of your deepest thoughts and feelings this week?

3. Whom do you admire most? Do they share deep aspects of themselves? How has that impacted you?

4. As you reflect on your life, when was a time you chose to be vulnerable with someone else? What did you notice about the connection and how you felt afterwards?

Based upon my observations and insights this week:

I will stop _____

_____.

I will start _____

_____.

I will continue _____

_____.

You are ENOUGH.

You ARE Worth It!

WEEK 33

Celebrate Your Feelings

We can't heal what we can't feel.

—Debbie Ford

Your emotions are great barometers of what's going on in your life. Whether you feel boredom and resentment or joy and satisfaction, your emotions tell you what is working for you and what isn't. Emotions have a life of their own. They will last as long as they will last. To try to control your emotions is futile. You cannot wish your feelings away. You can't always choose how you feel, but you can be aware of how you feel and choose how to respond to a situation and to others. It is actually something to celebrate. Many people are not in touch with their feelings.

Your opinions are your own. You can choose the actions you take. You are always in charge of where you place your attention. There is no way to manage another person's feelings or thoughts. Stay with your own process. Take a few deep breaths. By doing so, you create time and space for yourself to get centered again.

Anger, unexpressed in a healthy way, can be scary and very

destructive in relationships, as well as to your soul. Someone may have insulted you or provoked you. Remember what is truly irritating in such a circumstance is not the person who offended you. It is your judgment about how you are being treated. Anger can be like a gauge on the dashboard of your car. Pay attention. Be proactive. You may choose to set clear boundaries. If not honored, you may choose to leave the situation or relationship.

> *You can't always choose how you feel, but you can be aware of how you feel and choose how to respond to a situation and to others.*

I Am Worth It Next Steps:

1. Take an emotional barometer reading. How do you feel right now? Are you feeling down, upbeat, worried, or hopeful? Reflect on what those feelings may be telling you to do or choices you can make in different areas of your life.

2. Are you or are your feelings in the driver's seat of your life?

3. Write down some of the ways your feelings may be affecting others.

4. Scan your entire being. What are you feeling? Can you connect the feeling to a current situation?

5. Walking, singing, dancing, or getting into a project important to you can help to release and redirect the feelings impacting your life in a negative way. What resonates with you?

Based upon my observations and insights this week:

I will stop _____

_____.

I will start _____

_____.

I will continue _____

_____.

You are not your feelings. You have feelings. You can pause, discern, and decide what to do.

You ARE Worth It!

WEEK 34

Make the Conscious Choice to Forgive

Forgiveness is an act of the will, and the will can function regardless of the temperature of the heart.

—Corrie Ten Boom

"Forgive and forget" is a popular saying. To me, this phrase doesn't seem realistic or complete; however, I do think it's doable for most of us to forgive and then gently remember. Also, it's easier to forgive from your heart first, perhaps later finding the words to say out loud. The truth is, forgiveness is a choice. It is not a feeling; however, your feelings and energy will be affected by this powerful choice. To forgive means to relinquish your desire for revenge and retaliation. When you choose to forgive, you release the other person from his or her offenses, and release yourself from resentment and bitterness. Holding a grudge is like trying to hold a 500-pound rock. The effort required is enormous. You could be using the same amount of energy to do things to bring you joy and to meditate on thoughts to feed your soul.

It takes time to rebuild trust. You remember gently so you can learn from the situation, and make adjustments in relationships and the direction of your life.

Let go of your anger. It does not contribute to the process of forgiveness. Depersonalize the situation. If you look closely at the wrongdoing, you'll usually find it has nothing to do with you and everything to do with the other person. Removing yourself from the equation makes it easier for you to rise above the situation. You move forward and lighten up.

Forgiving yourself for a mistake can be the greatest challenge of all for many of us. You cannot change what you did or failed to do. You can ask forgiveness of another person, and then decide on a different course of action for the future.

> *When you choose to forgive, you release the other person from his or her offenses, and release yourself from resentment and bitterness.*

I Am Worth It Next Steps:

1. Think of a grudge you may be holding. Write the feelings of your grudge in a letter, and then toss it into the fireplace or shred it. Do this while looking at a lit candle with soothing music playing in the background.
2. Is there an area in your life where it is important to forgive yourself?
3. Reflect upon times and situations in which you made the conscious choice to forgive. What were the benefits and impact of doing so?

4. Is there anyone in your life right now whom you still cannot forgive, and you hold this in your heart? Do you think it is time to beginning working on this?

Based upon my observations and insights this week:

I will stop _____

_____.

I will start _____

_____.

I will continue _____

_____.

You choose to forgive often. You are a healer, and you call forth peace from others and from the world.

You ARE Worth It!

WEEK 35

Honor Your Grief

The grief within me has its own heartbeat. It has its own life, its own song. Part of me wants to resist the rhythms of my grief, yet as I surrender to the song, I learn to listen deep within myself.

—Alan Wolfelt

When faced with a loss, crisis, or life-changing event, you are suddenly thrust into a new world, a world that is unfamiliar, and this can seem daunting or frightening. It is a world of intense, unsettling, and at times, even conflicting feelings of loss, anger, depression, loneliness, fear, frustration, and desperation. Many life changes involve loss, including loss of dreams. You grieve the endings, be they the endings of relationships or careers. One of the most painful losses you experience is the death of a loved one. It is an event over which you have no control. Grief is a natural, active process during which you experience intense feelings, revisit memories, and adjust to life without your loved one.

There is no "right" way to grieve. Elizabeth Kubler-Ross, a psychiatrist, has identified five stages of grieving: denial, anger, bargaining, depression, and acceptance. As you know, these stages do not follow methodically in order, and certainly have different degrees of intensity. There is no timetable. The ups and downs while grieving can be unpredictable. Knowing this can be helpful. This is a journey of the heart and soul. Do it your way. Everyone deals with loss differently. Don't let others influence how you should mourn or feel.

The support of family and friends is more important than ever during times of grief and loss. Many of my therapy clients over the years have benefited from various grief support groups offered in the community, often at churches. There is no "right" time to attend. Give the group a try for at least two times before deciding not to return. It could have been an "off" time for the group or "off" time for you. Perhaps the chemistry of another group will be a better fit for you.

Experiencing grief can impact your life in meaningful ways. As your healing journey continues, you may become more compassionate toward others. In time, you may find yourself filled with gratitude for the other wonderful things present in your life. Forgiveness of yourself and others may become a priority. You may decide to live life more fully, realizing that life and relationships are indeed precious.

> *Grieving is a journey of the heart and soul.*
> *Do it your way.*

I Am Worth It Next Steps:

1. Reflecting on your life, what is the earliest loss you remember experiencing?

2. How did you feel, and what was most helpful to you in your grieving process?

3. What is your greatest loss to-date? What helped you cope, and what did you learn or are you learning?

4. Whom do you know who has experienced a loss of some type recently? When and how will you reach out to that person?

Based upon my observations and insights this week:

I will stop _____

_____.

I will start _____

_____.

I will continue _____

_____.

Be in the moment. You will find your way. You can honor your process. It is right for you.

You ARE Worth It!

WEEK 36

Respect Differences

I believe we are here for each other, not against each other. Everything comes from an understanding that you are a gift in my life—whoever you are, whatever our differences.

—John Denver

Choosing to spend time understanding someone who differs significantly from you can be a challenge, as well as a rich opportunity while you are expanding your horizons and perspectives on life. You may have no experience with the person's ways of life or customs; however, being curious and understanding of differences is important to maintaining harmony in your relationships. Spend time getting to know that person. Ask questions about that person's customs and traditions. You will discover similarities as well as differences.

Accept things with which you do not agree. Being respectful of individuals' differences doesn't always mean agreeing with them. If you have a difference of opinion that simply can't be overcome, move past this disagreement, looking at it as only a difference of opinions, not a matter of right or wrong. Instead of fighting against differences, embrace them. Use the experience to learn and grow as a person.

When you respect each person—regardless of differences in opinion and beliefs—families, schools, and communities will be safer places in which to live. Mutual respect is the foundation for healthy relationships and collaboration.

I love to watch children play. They spontaneously interact with each other as human beings who have much in common. It seems they have not yet learned to look for differences. Children teach us wise lessons, and give us new perspectives to consider.

> *Instead of fighting against differences, embrace them.*
> *Use the experience to learn and grow as a person.*

I Am Worth It Next Steps:

1. Reflect upon a relationship you value where there are indeed differences present. How do you contribute to this relationship to keep it alive?

2. What is a gift you have received from another person as you explored and accepted the differences between you?

3. How does mutual respect impact your feeling of worthiness?

4. Who might you reach out to this week in spite of some differences you experience?

Based upon my observations and insights this week:

I will stop _____

_____.

I will start _____

_____.

I will continue _____

_____.

You continue to make a positive impact in the world as you accept people for the value they hold as a human being, regardless of differences.

You ARE Worth It!

WEEK 37

Ask for What You Want and Need

If you don't go after what you want, you'll never have it. If you don't ask, the answer is always no. If you don't step forward, you're always in the same place.

—Nora Roberts

If you ask for what you truly desire, then you may be ridiculed. Some people may shame you and call you self-centered. Hold fast to the essence of who you are and what you most want. It very well can be a part of your soul's purpose.

Needing and asking for help does not mean you are helpless. It actually may signify you are very healthy and clear. While on the receiving end, you might also learn invaluable lessons about how to help others when they reach out to you.

Perhaps you have spent a lifetime pleasing others. It may feel foreign to consider your own wants and needs. However, each time you choose *not to ask* for what you need or to confront someone who treats you poorly, you chip away at your self-esteem and confidence. As you begin to honor your feelings and needs, others might label you as selfish. You may even feel selfish at first. However, you will find as you begin to respect yourself more that you set better boundaries, and others may also respect you more. As you acknowledge and honor your own needs, your authentic relationships will deepen, and you will attract new people into your life to replace those you may outgrow. A new energy and confidence come as you practice this more.

> *Each time you choose not to ask for what you need or to confront someone who treats you poorly, you chip away at your self-esteem and confidence.*

I Am Worth It Next Steps:

1. At this time in your life, how comfortable are you at asking for what you want and need from others?
2. Are there certain situations or relationships in your life where you find this more difficult?
3. What is getting in your way?
4. What do you have inside of you that can help you be more assertive?

Based upon my observations and insights this week:

I will stop _____

_____.

I will start _____

_____.

I will continue _____

_____.

You have the right to ask for the things you want and need.

You ARE Worth It!

WEEK 38

Offer Compassion

Until he extends the circle of his compassion to all living things, man will not himself find peace.

—Albert Schweitzer

Compassion is the active expression of acceptance for the world and people just as they are. It encompasses a state of mind where there is no judgment about a situation or a person. You let go of expectations about how the world should be.

Showing more compassion toward yourself and others can increase your happiness, health, and well-being. Compassion is essential for inner peace, emotional stability, and mental clarity. It lifts your spirit, opens your heart, and builds a bridge, rather than a wall, between you and others.

When you have been around someone weeping and grieving over the loss of a relationship, a job, property, or even a loved one, it is important to honor what is going on in her life by showing compassion and acknowledging what is going on. You might say something such as, "I imagine you are feeling deep sadness." On the other hand, sometimes the best action you can take to help relieve the emotional suffering of another is to be present with your attention on the person and say nothing. Being compassionate involves understanding the suffering of another without feeling sorrow or pity or taking on their pain.

If you have a pattern of indulging in self-pity, redirect your energy into helping someone else. Feeling another person's suffering, and doing something about it, lessens your own woes considerably. Be gentle with yourself. When you are going through a tough time, treat yourself with the same compassion you would show a good friend.

During difficult circumstances, think about the times in your past when you have overcome a hurdle. Call for the same strengths now that saw you through hardships in the past. You have what is needed inside of you.

> *Being compassionate involves understanding the suffering of another without feeling sorrow or pity or taking on their pain.*

I Am Worth It Next Steps:

1. How often are you compassionate toward yourself?
2. How quickly are you able to move from judgment of others to compassion for others?
3. What are the gifts you give and receive by being compassionate?
4. To whom will you reach out this week?

Based upon my observations and insights this week:

I will stop _____

_____.

I will start _____

_____.

I will continue _____

_____.

You are a gift to others and can be present to them as no one else can in the same way.

You ARE Worth It!

WEEK 39

Have Fun, Relax, and Enjoy Life

We do not quit playing because we grow old. We grow old because we quit playing.

—Oliver Wendell Holmes

We all know people who seem much older than their years. Likewise, we all know people who seem much younger in spirit. Have you ever thought about what makes the difference? It all comes back to one thing: fun. If you maintain a sense of humor and zest for life, you will always be young at heart. In addition, scientific research shows that play is critical to your performance on every level and also in reducing stress. It is vital to problem-solving, creativity, and building relationships. Play decreases your stress, energizes your body, and nourishes your spirit. It is how you recharge your batteries.

Do you remember stomping your way through a puddle in bright yellow boots ... or no boots at all? Do you also remember squishing mud between your fingers to make "pies?" Somewhere along the way, puddles changed from paradise to nuisances to avoid. Imagine the fun if, once in a while, you jump right in and get a little dirty. You will regain the magic when you view the world lightheartedly. Loosen up and jump in a pile of autumn leaves, run through a sprinkler, or ride a bike through puddles after a rainstorm. Observe children closely because they can mentor you in this area, regardless of your age. My grandchildren continue to teach me and show me options. They remind me of when ….

Rediscover the world. If you feel you lost something while growing up, be creative as to how to recreate and experience it. Curiosity and the happiness that comes from simple, earthy pleasures can be found again if you are ready to explore options. Laugh often, especially at yourself.

Explore interesting experiences, whether it is scuba diving, Zumba, sushi, or samba lessons. Make time for trying something new. If you have given up an activity or hobby because you think you are too old for it, think again. If it continues to make you feel good, don't stop. The best way to stay young is to stay active in a life filled with challenges and adventures.

> *Imagine the fun if, once in a while, you jump right in and get a little dirty.*

I Am Worth It Next Steps:

1. What activities will bring more laughter into your life?
2. Plan a fun excursion with friends. It will lift your spirit and remind you of "playtime," no matter what your age.
3. What would you really love to do and experience, even

if others may not understand and think you might have lost your mind?

4. What will you commit to doing for yourself this week in this area of fun and relaxation?

Based upon my observations and insights this week:

I will stop _____

_____.

I will start _____

_____.

I will continue _____

_____.

You are fun. The world would not be the same without YOU. Keep replenishing yourself.

You ARE Worth It!

WEEK 40

Start Building Your Legacy

When I grow old, I want to know I've left something behind ... not as an artist, but as a human being who loves and gives and tends and helps other human beings. To do that is to walk in beauty.

—Mary Monez

Legacy is defined as "something received from an ancestor or predecessor from the past" (Webster). It also means how someone is remembered and what contributions she or he made while alive. You can write and shape your own legacy. How do you want to be remembered?

- Is it for your smile, your sense of humor, or your wit?
- Is it for your prowess with sports or other competition?
- Is it for your creativity, your intelligence, or your ability to get things done?
- Is it based on your accomplishments at work or in the community?
- Is it for your involvement as a parent, grandparent, significant other, relative, or friend?

While you cannot fully control your legacy and how you are remembered, you are more likely to achieve the desired results if you create them rather than moving randomly through life without direction or purpose. If you want some hope of being remembered in certain ways, then these memories are more likely to occur if you plan for them, be it in the area of relationships, achievements, or contributions you make to the world. Some people are called to create large projects and even movements. Others are not. Once again, it is not about comparing your legacy with someone else's. Be true to you.

As you reflect on this, you may record your thoughts, and review them occasionally, either in a journal or a verbal recording. Review it on a regular basis, such as once a year on your birthday. Create a plan for how you are going to achieve it in terms of short-term and longer-term strategies. Your likelihood of success is greater when you have a plan.

You may choose to write a personal legacy letter to share what has been most important in your life with the people who have been most important in your life. Speak from your heart in your own voice. The words you write can bring a deeper meaning to your life in the present, as well as create healing in your relationships. It is intended to be shared with loved ones while you are still alive. Some possible areas of reflection are: values and life lessons; special memories and cherished moments; spiritual beliefs; regrets and forgiveness; future hopes and wishes; and expressions of gratitude, love, and blessings.

> *You can write and shape your own legacy.*
> *How do you want to be remembered?*

I Am Worth It Next Steps:

1. What do you value most in your life at the moment? How can you express this to others?
2. What is the most significant lesson your life experience has taught you?
3. What are three moments or memories in your life you especially cherish? If they involve other people, somehow communicate that to them this week.
4. What has given you strength to make it through difficult times in your life?

Based upon my observations and insights this week:

I will stop _____

_____.

I will start _____

_____.

I will continue _____

_____.

You are a remarkable person and a true gift to others. Be even more of who you are.

You ARE Worth It!

WEEK 41

Believe in Your Dreams

Believe in your dreams. They were given to you for a reason.
—Katrina Mayer

Like flowers, dreams are both beautiful and fragile. With careful nurturing, dreams grow strong and are able to withstand setbacks and failure. If you let your faith be overwhelmed by fear and doubts, your dreams may falter and wither away. Keep your dreams alive by allowing belief, not fear, to grow ever stronger in your heart.

The daydreaming mind asks, "What if?" and "What would happen if?" Let your curiosity and creativity come out to play. Those who dream or indulge in fantasy are often chided for being "foolish." Yet if you stop letting your imagination run free, you may stop seeing new, creative possibilities for yourself, and life can become grey and stagnant. Dreams often come at the most ordinary times. If you pay attention, dreams can change your life as you pursue them.

Allow your dreams to be heard, regardless of the risk of embarrassment. Share them with others, as well as repeating them often to yourself. Work towards releasing your dreams by acting on them any way possible. Resources will appear. At the end of the day, you must be loyal to yourself by never giving up on your dream. Ultimately, trust yourself. Believe in yourself. Believe in your potential. Remember the dreams you gave up on, and rekindle your passion for those dreams. Imagine how you will feel when you achieve them. If they are important to you, nothing will stand in your way.

If a dream makes your heart beat faster, gives you something to look forward to, and adds an exciting dimension to your life—go for it. You are bound to learn something and have fun along the way.

> *Keep your dreams alive by allowing belief, not fear, to grow ever stronger in your heart.*

I Am Worth It Next Steps:

1. What are three things you do well? Reflect on them whenever you feel yourself in a mental fog. This exercise can give you the powerful reminder that you need to keep your dreams in sight.

2. What is one thing you have always wanted to do? Say it out loud, which may be the first step to getting started. A dream is a dream. There is no such thing as doing "it" perfectly.

3. What is your closet dream, the one that seems so

unreachable, so crazy you can't share it with anyone, such as singing in a band, running for office, or going back to college at your current age?

4. What is a dream you pursued that did come true? How did you contribute to the result?

Based upon my observations and insights this week:

I will stop _____

_____.

I will start _____

_____.

I will continue _____

_____.

You are wise and can delight in the dreams that come forth within you.

You ARE Worth It!

WEEK 42

Hold on to Hope

Hope is the thing with feathers that perches in the soul and sings the tune without the words and never stops at all.

—Emily Dickinson

Just as oxygen fills your lungs, hope inflates your spirit with the essence of what you need to live and prosper. Hope restores your belief in the goodness of others and yourself. It sustains you during hard times. It provides comfort through a trying day. Hope gives your life a sense of purpose. When you have hope, you are breathing fresh, new life.

Hope is an optimistic attitude of mind based on the expectation of positive outcomes related to events and circumstances in one's life or the world at large. Hope comes into its own when a crisis looms, opening you to new creative possibilities. It is also linked to the existence of a goal, which is combined with a determined plan for reaching that goal.

What gives you hope? Perhaps it is the birth of a baby, the sun breaking through a stormy sky, a happily married couple. Use those images to renew your spirit when you need it.

Pay attention to times when you seem to lose hope. It is possible you are burned out because of extreme levels of stress in your life. It is also possible you are experiencing untreated depression, which can be very subtle at first. Pay attention to the presence of these symptoms: feelings of helplessness or hopelessness, loss of interest in daily activities, appetite or weight change, sleep changes, anger or irritability, loss of energy, self-loathing, reckless behavior, or concentration problems. If you have a combination of several of these, and they denote a change from what is normal for you, talk with a therapist or see your medical doctor. As a psychologist, I know depression is both real and treatable.

> *When you have hope, you are breathing fresh, new life.*

I Am Worth It Next Steps:

1. What gives you hope? Who gives you hope?
2. Reflect on a time when something seemed impossible, but you saw hope, and it worked out.
3. Is there a connection for you between hope and faith?
4. Who in your life do you know might need a little extra hope? How will you reach out to that person?

Based upon my observations and insights this week:

I will stop _____

_____.

I will start _____

_____.

I will continue _____

_____.

You bring hope to others because of who you are as a person.

You ARE Worth It!

WEEK 43

Take More Risks

And the day came when the risk to remain tight in a bud was more painful than the risk it took to blossom.

—Anaïs Nin

When you hear the word "risk," what do you imagine? Further, how does it make you feel? Frankly, most of us are terrified of the word "risk," as its very definition operates outside of our comfort zone. A risk embodies the possibility of failure, disappointment, or something bad happening. Yet taking risks stimulates your innate need to grow. It's nearly impossible to live fully without taking risks. The probability of a new and "risky" experience or relationship often keeps you from doing the very thing your soul needs—to evolve.

Are there areas in your life where you feel as though you are stuck in a rut—where life seems stagnant? Something is off when you find yourself no longer expanding your *reserve* of understanding and experiences. Often, this leads to becoming spiritually depleted. When you find yourself feeling this way, it is time to play a little and discover what it is you need to reinvigorate your spiritual and emotional growth.

Risks can be drastic transformational endeavors: starting a new business, choosing to love someone again, or ending a toxic relationship. Or maybe a risk you need to take is as simple as introducing yourself to a new hobby or conquering your bucket list once and for all.

Now is the time. What are you waiting for? When it comes to taking risks, don't think, "What happens if this doesn't work?" Instead think, "I'm taking this risk because I need to and want to. The outcome, whether good or bad, will strengthen my resolve and make me better. I look forward to meeting 'me' on the other side of this."

Put yourself out there. Take a ballroom dancing class, propose something new at work, or sing karaoke. Feeling fear, but forging ahead anyway, is the best way to overcome it. Speak your mind. If holding back at work or in relationships has become a habit, take steps to break it. There is a chance you will be disappointed; however, you will not know if you do not try. Think about what you can and will learn.

> *It's nearly impossible to live fully without taking risks.*

I Am Worth It Next Steps:
1. What is something you have never attempted and are ready to take on now?
2. Move outside your comfort zone and do something this

week that stretches you. See how good it feels, and do it again.

3. Make a list of five risks you have taken in your life. Let yourself feel proud of your courage and confidence.

4. Whom do you respect who is a risk-taker? What can you learn from this person?

Based upon my observations and insights this week:

I will stop _____

_____.

I will start _____

_____.

I will continue _____

_____.

You are wise and creative, and you will know what risks to take next.

You ARE Worth It!

WEEK 44

Increase Your Confidence

I was once afraid of people saying, 'Who does she think she is?'
Now I have the courage to stand and say, "This is who I am."
—Oprah Winfrey

The words "confidence" and "self-confidence" are often used interchangeably. Distinguishing their qualities is important to claiming your courage. *Confidence* can be defined as a feeling or consciousness of one's power or of reliance on one's circumstances, faith, or belief that one will act in the right or effective way. It is a general realization of one's abilities and one's belief in others, referring to situations and circumstances "out there." ("I am confident everything will work out for the best.")

Self-confidence is a belief in oneself and in one's strengths and capabilities. It is specific to the person, that he/she will be able to handle what needs to be done. Closely tied to your self-esteem, it is a kind of trust in yourself. ("I am confident I can prepare a presentation and speak to the large group of people who have registered.")

We need both confidence and self-confidence. They are two sides of the same coin.

Do you ever wonder why some people are more confident than others? Confidence is learned. Highly confident people take ownership of their mistakes and recognize them as opportunities to learn. They do not blame the outside world. Rather than just assume, they ask, and then take action. They problem-solve and get things done rather than making judgments or assuming the worst.

Highly confident people take care of their mind and body. They don't get stuck; they get creative. Confident people are real and authentic. They embrace change and celebrate others' successes. Confident people embrace time alone as an opportunity to reflect and create, and they do not need to fill every available moment with external stimuli. They take care of themselves first, so they have the power to take care of others.

To have confidence, you will create a reality you can depend upon. When you have confidence within you, it produces a positive energy, which quiets doubt, worry, fear, and negative expectations. It has a profound effect on you and others. Attitudes are contagious. Act the part. Even if you are not confident, you can act as though you are. It will have a positive effect on those around you. In time, it will eventually become a self-fulfilling prophecy. Take pride in yourself. It helps you feel as if nothing can stop you.

> *We need both confidence and self-confidence.*
> *They are two sides of the same coin.*

I Am Worth It Next Steps:

1. Can you think of a time you "faked it" until you "made it?" What did you learn in the process? Can you do it again? When?

2. Reflect on two areas or situations in your life when you feel very confident. What are they, and how do you feel as you see yourself in them?

3. Reflect upon two areas or situations in which you *do not feel* confident. What are they, and how do you feel as you see yourself in them?

4. Who in your life could use a little more encouragement? What will you do to encourage her or him this week?

Based upon my observations and insights this week:

I will stop _____

_____.

I will start _____

_____.

I will continue _____

_____.

You have the strengths, skills, and confidence to make your next step happen.

You ARE Worth It!

WEEK 45

Seek Self-Awareness

Self-awareness is value-free. It isn't scary. It doesn't imply that you will subject yourself to needless pain.

—Deepak Chopra

Self-awareness is the first step to changing and reclaiming your life. Without knowledge of yourself, you would have no hope for conscious, positive change. Change is essential to growth. We are all perfectly imperfect. Your life is your classroom. You can use it to grow and change—to become more attuned to and in harmony with everything around us. Awareness is the key.

Self-awareness describes a situation where the light of awareness is turned on yourself.

It is about knowing your own emotions, understanding your thinking patterns, and choosing what thinking pattern to use in certain situations. Self-awareness includes understanding your strengths and weaknesses, as well as knowing what motivates you and what you want out of life. The motivation for breaking bad habits comes from the detrimental effects the bad habits are having in your life. The self-motivation to change also comes from a vivid awareness of what you want for yourself and for your future, recognizing you simply won't be able to have it if you do not leave your bad habits behind.

Also of extreme importance is the awareness of how your thoughts, choices, and actions impact other people. Some people go through life without this awareness, which can have devastating consequences in personal and professional relationships. You are the only one responsible.

Self-awareness is your ability to notice yourself in the present moment. It is a good measure of "presence." Being present with your body can bring awareness of many things. A gut feeling may alert you to something that is not quite right; the flow of blood in your veins can awaken you to the simple joy of being alive; a shiver down your spine may let you know you are connected to a truth. Noticing this internal activity as it happens is a manifestation of self-awareness. It helps you keep up with life as it happens, including constant choices the present moment brings.

> ### *Self-awareness: You are the only one responsible.*

I Am Worth It Next Steps:

1. Spend three minutes at various times during the day this week to become acutely aware of every physical movement you make, noticing what happens as you do. Make no analysis. Be in the moment.

2. As you notice people this week, look at each person with

complete openness, with no story attached, and no pre-conceived idea. Notice the person, and be aware of the noticing.

3. What are you most aware of as being your greatest challenge at this time in your life?

4. As you reflect on your life, what are the greatest gifts you have received from your own self-awareness?

Based upon my observations and insights this week:

I will stop _____

_____.

I will start _____

_____.

I will continue _____

_____.

You are wise and will continue to be self-aware, making changes as you go.

You ARE Worth It!

WEEK 46

Celebrate Your Successes

The more you praise and celebrate your life, the more there is in life to celebrate.

—Oprah Winfrey

How many times have you found yourself working hard to accomplish something in your life—imagining the incredible pride you will feel and the celebrations you will have once you reach your goal—only to let the accomplishment or event pass unceremoniously?

What happened? Is it possible you were too busy planning your next mission to soak in your present success? Hard work without celebration is a burnout waiting to happen. You need to have balance. Lingering in the afterglow of your success, regardless of its size, is almost as important as accomplishing your goal. When you celebrate your achievements, you send out a signal that you are happy with yourself and the outcome of your efforts. By doing so, you build upon your next success.

Some concrete benefits of recognizing and acknowledging your successes:

- Builds loyalty to the outcome of your goal or desire.
- Increases your positive motivation.

- Pumps up inner confidence and develops a hopeful attitude.
- Nurtures a growing belief that you can have what you want.
- Reinforces your desired behaviors.
- Helps you stay positively focused despite short-term setbacks.
- Allows you time to review what got you to where you are now.

The meaning of true success is different for each of you and will perhaps change at different times in your life. You must figure out what success means to you before you can achieve it. Know your "why," and create a plan. Keep success journals where you record your top three successes for the day before going to bed. Combine that with your gratitude reflections, and you will sleep very well.

> *You must figure out what success means to you before you can achieve it.*

I Am Worth It Next Steps:

1. What is your definition of success for yourself at this time in your life?
2. Review your achievements. What made you the proudest?
3. What do you need to do to set yourself up to experience more success?

4. How will you celebrate your successes this week?

Based upon my observations and insights this week:

I will stop _____

_____.

I will start _____

_____.

I will continue _____

_____.

You are worth celebrating every day.

You ARE Worth It!

WEEK 47

Share Your Gifts with Others

The greatest good you can do for another is not just to share your riches, but to reveal to him his own.

—Benjamin Disraeli

You came into the world with your own set of unique gifts. You have continued to develop them and have added more to your essence. They vary in form and function. You have certain ways of being, as well as skill, talents, and personality traits that come naturally from your authentic being.

At times it is easier to focus on your shortcomings or what you *do not* have when compared to others. As a result, you may hide some of your gifts and let them lie dormant in your soul. This is a waste of time and energy. You rob others of experiencing the gifts you bring to help enhance their lives. This perspective depletes you and makes you feel small. When you do become aware of what you have to give, you feel whole.

When you honor your gifts, you honor yourself and everyone around you. Sharing your gifts with others, no matter how small or how large, is an expression of love and abundance. Your personal power is defined in part by your gifts. To use your talents is to demonstrate to the world that you understand yourself and are attuned to your capabilities, while positively touching the lives of others. You may bring the gift of hospitality, organization, clear communication, creating beauty, music, kindness, and fun, to name just a few. Each gift you bring is enrichment to the lives of others.

While at my grandson's birthday party recently, I observed a group of nine children, ages 5-11, run, play, and interact. Their unique talents and gifts were evident. I have seen them grow and mature over the years. The combination makes for a very full, enriching life experience. It will be interesting to see how they continue to use their gifts in the world. They already make a difference. I also closely observed the adults of varying ages who were present, and I was aware of their unique gifts and how they were using them in the world. It was a rich experience.

> ***When you honor your gifts, you honor yourself and everyone around you.***

I Am Worth It Next Steps:

1. Did you decide (or learn from others) early in life there were negative consequences to feelings of confidence and owning your gifts and talents?

2. What three of your gifts make a contribution and impact in the world?

3. How comfortable are you owning and celebrating your gifts?

4. Who will you acknowledge this week for the life-enriching gifts they shared with you?

Based upon my observations and insights this week:

I will stop _____

_____.

I will start _____

_____.

I will continue _____

_____.

You are magnificent. The gifts you bring to the world make a profound difference.

You ARE Worth It!

WEEK 48

Own Your Happiness

A happy person is not a person in a certain set of circumstances, but rather a person with a certain set of attitudes.

—Hugh Downs

The words happiness and joy (see Week 49 for joy) are often used interchangeably; however, there can be a difference. Happiness is an emotion in which a person experiences feelings ranging from contentment and satisfaction to bliss and intense pleasure. It can be temporary, if based on external circumstances such as observing or doing a particular thing. Happiness can become a part of the fiber of your life. It is your birthright.

If you want to be truly happy, cultivate indifference about what others think of you. It doesn't matter if they believe you are foolish, stupid, or even intelligent. Some things are within your power to control, and some things are not. Become conscious of how you view yourself. It is one thing over which you do have control. When you intentionally decide to experience more happiness each day, you do. The "price" is also right. It involves a conscious choice on your part.

Use your energy wisely. No one can hurt you unless you allow it. You injure yourself when you think you have been treated unkindly. Decide how you will treat others, like neighbors, family members, and authority figures. Do that in spite of their behavior toward you, while setting clear boundaries where appropriate. Decide how you will treat yourself.

Let go of your conditional thinking, such as, "If I quit my job, I won't be able to pay my bills." Be aware of the following

formula: *If I_____, then_____*

will happen. Or, *If_____, then_____*

_____, and I will be happy. Happiness is an internal state of being only you can create and maintain.

Laughter is both the result of and a cause for loving yourself more intensely. How great it is to laugh with others and to laugh at yourself, enjoying the delight of acknowledging your humanity. It is also good for the health of your body, mind, and spirit.

As Og Mandino says, "Man is most comical when he takes himself too seriously."

> ***Become conscious of how you view yourself.***
> ***It is one thing over which you do have control.***

I Am Worth It Next Steps:

1. When in life are you happiest?
2. Is it possible to feel sad about some things while still being happy about others? Can these two feelings co-exist?
3. Who in your life would benefit from you sharing some of your happiness with them?
4. Notice this week when and where you experience happiness in yourself and others. What kind of energy is present? How can you create more of this state of being?

Based upon my observations and insights this week:

I will stop _____

_____.

I will start _____

_____.

I will continue _____

_____.

Be the bright shining light you are again and again and again.

You ARE Worth It!

WEEK 49

Find Your Joy

Joy is the holy fire that keeps our purpose warm and our intelligence aglow.

—Helen Keller

Joy is more than happiness. It is a state of being. Joy is the WOW experience of just being alive. It is an emotional pattern and an abiding sense of happiness. It is the fiber of your soul. It is a part of your essence. Your access to it never vanishes. You experience it in intense moments, such as when you fulfill a goal, achieve success, feel connected with others and are a part of something special, and see the beauty in the world and in those you love.

Joy tempers moments or seasons of sadness. It brings a confident expectation that the sun will soon return, piercing the darkness caused by passing clouds. Joy is the result of faith, hope, and love. It is a choice, and sometimes it takes conscious focus.

Joyful people are typically happy. They smile and laugh a lot. They see problems as opportunities. Joyful people are grateful for what they have, enjoy it thoroughly and do not fear it running out. They walk with a spring in their step and light-heartedness that is contagious. When they do something, they do it with zest and vitality. Joy empowers a person to be loving, kind, and gentle. Joyful people remember the playful child inside of them. They express gratitude daily. They are also generous with their time, talent, and resources. They forgive daily.

Whatever heartbreaking times you have experienced in your life, be it betrayal, financial hardship, divorce, or dashed dreams, you can return to the baseline of your being—the supreme gift of being alive. You can still celebrate the joy to be here, connected, animated, breathing, blessed, to be open, to have what was, what's left, and what's coming.

What brings you joy may be different than for another person. Spend time identifying experiences that contribute to your joy. It may be being in nature. For others it is dancing, singing, traveling, exercising, volunteering, meditating, or creating something to bring them joy. Someone cannot take your joy away from you. It is yours to keep, enjoy, and share with others.

> *Joy is the result of faith, hope, and love. It is a choice, and sometimes it takes conscious focus.*

I Am Worth It Next Steps:

1. Name three things that bring you joy in your life. Focus on one you will experience this week.

2. Are you satisfied with the amount of joy you feel on a daily basis? If not, what are choices over which you have control?

3. Who is someone you respect and admire who is truly a joyful person? What do you notice and experience being with them? How can you incorporate that into your life?

4. Do something unexpected this week to bring joy into someone's life. Who will you choose, and what is your plan?

Based upon my observations and insights this week:

I will stop _____

_____.

I will start _____

_____.

I will continue _____

_____.

You are pure joy at your core. Continue to tap into it and share it with others.

You ARE Worth It!

WEEK 50

Discover Your Spiritual Path

When your soul awakens, you begin to truly inherit your life. You leave the kingdom of fake surfaces, repetitive talk and weary roles and slip deeper into the true adventure of who you are and who you are called to become.

—John O'Donohue

Your spiritual path is unique and significant to you. There is not a right or wrong way to create this or to be. Each path is personal and unique.

Are you feeling there *has to be* more to life than what you are currently experiencing? Are you seeking more meaning? More joy? More peace? You may have experienced a recent trauma or loss, a deep hurt still causing you pain, or a feeling of emptiness. Old ways of coping don't seem to work now.

Your spiritual path is beckoning. It may be the road less traveled—until now. The key is to look within and beyond at the same time. But where do you start? If you are faith-based, you can pray and be open to the words, feelings, or impressions that may be given to you. If you are looking for direction from a learned person, then ask your priest/rabbi/pastor or a good friend—or whomever you feel is the right person, one who will truly listen to you without judgment and will help you to see both your gifts and your possible journey ahead.

Once you give voice to your intention, you will receive affirmations about your path. They may come in the form of insightful comments from a trusted friend or advisor, a quote or passage in something you are reading, a perspective from nature, or even a dream. Stay open. Try on the ideas. Look at the signposts you are given, even though they may seem illogical. At the same time, trust your own inner voice and intention. If it feels right to you and reaffirms your direction, take action. If not, trust those feelings to know this *is not* your way forward. Accept guidance from others while also being your own best guide on the journey.

Spirituality is a critical component of the overall concept of wellness. Find what is true in your heart, be present to it, and follow the path, knowing *this is your journey*.

> *Once you give voice to your intention, you will receive affirmations about your path.*

I Am Worth It Next Steps:

1. Have you ever judged another person because you did not understand his or her spiritual path? What lesson can you learn from this choice?

2. What three foundational pieces of your spiritual path

comfort you and bring you peace?

3. Who in your life has been a significant mentor on your spiritual path? What did you learn from this person? Contact her if you are able to do so and let her know the impact she had in your life.

4. Who can you reach out to this week that could use some encouragement as they walk their spiritual path?

Based upon my observations and insights this week:

I will stop _____

_____.

I will start _____

_____.

I will continue _____

_____.

You are a wise spiritual person who brings peace, love, and joy to those around you.

You ARE Worth It!

WEEK 51

Be Yourself

This above all; to thine own self be true.

—William Shakespeare

Being the normal child, you wanted to be loved and to fit in and belong. You paid attention to what pleased your parents, and you made interpretations about how you should be and the roles you should play in order to be loved and have significance.

If you were recognized for exceeding your parents' expectations, such as in school, you might have decided that you needed to continue to be a high performer in order to have worth and be loved as an adult. If you were acknowledged and encouraged every time you followed your parents' directives, you might have grown up as a conformist, believing it would not be in your best self-interest to go against the norm in any group, like your family, social circle, or organization. A variation of this is striving to please others, not considering your own wants and needs. Compromising who you are to please others is accepting less than you deserve. You get the idea. The question you are hopefully asking yourself along the way is, "How is this working in my life now. Who am I?" It is easy to lose one's true self and essence along the way.

Find yourself and define yourself on your terms. You can't be yourself if you don't know, understand, and accept yourself first. Take time to reflect on what you value, and what makes up the essence of who you are. Think about your choices. What kinds of things would you like or not like to do? Act accordingly. Honor your truth, and trust yourself.

Avoid focusing on your past errors and mistakes. Highlight the lessons you have learned, and continue to grow. Own up to your own imperfections. Doing so can bring great freedom and peace. Stop caring about how people perceive you. Pay attention to the opinions of people who genuinely wish you well and who support you in the goals and dreams you have for your life.

Be in your own corner. Develop and express your individuality. Follow your own style. When you feel anxious or insecure, tell yourself what you would tell a good friend. Point out your amazing qualities and strengths. Trust in yourself. Treat yourself as you would your own best friend.

Compromising who you are to please others is accepting less than you deserve.
However, you can't be yourself if you don't know, understand, and accept yourself first.

I Am Worth It Next Steps:

1. What qualities and strengths best describe you right now? For example: friendly, loving, strong, kind, or loyal, to name just a few.
2. What are three things you really like to do? What will you focus on this week?
3. As you check in with your spirit, how do you authentically want to show up in the world? What is your plan?
4. Reflect on a time in the past few months when you were truly yourself. What did you notice, and what was the impact for you and others?

Based upon my observations and insights this week:

I will stop _____

_____.

I will start _____

_____.

I will continue _____

_____.

You bring magnificent gifts and blessings to others and to yourself by being who you authentically are.

You ARE Worth It!

WEEK 52

Live Fully Alive

Life is for living! And living is an experience in growth and unfoldment. It is not so important what happens around us or even to us. What counts is what happens in us.

—Eric Butterworth

Say a resounding "YES" to being alive. Continue to educate yourself. If something grabs your interest, follow through on it. Attend a class or lecture that sounds appealing. Share your enthusiasm with others. For instance, if you have seen a terrific show or read a book you enjoyed, tell your friends about it. You might be lighting the fire of curiosity in their lives. The more actively you build your enthusiasm, the easier life flows.

Who and what inspires you? Inspiration provides a burst of energy that attunes you to your inner knowing. It connects you to what's possible, breathing life into your vision. Instead of struggling with what you do not have a say in, focus on living with integrity and honoring yourself and others. If you do, the whole world around you will benefit. Imagine and know you are worthy of living happily and abundantly in harmony with yourself and others. Stay close to those things making you feel glad you are alive. Let the best of everything come to you effortlessly. Inspiration is the spark that ignites passion, purpose, and possibilities. When you are inspired, you naturally feel happier, energized, and motivated. Be the person you were created to be. Do your work. Play and have fun. Continuously nourish your spirit. Continue to give to others in ways that you know are healthy and life-giving.

- Choose to be loving and kind to each person you encounter.
- Choose to be joyful, even in the midst of difficulty.
- Choose to be peaceful, even in times of adversity.
- Choose to be patient when your patience is tested.
- Choose to be gentle when you are tempted to be harsh.
- Choose to be grateful in spite of challenges.

The combination of all these choices is a blessing to all.

You are in the driver's seat of your life with many people and resources available to you. Now you are at the end of this 52-week journey, and I hope you know you are worthy of love and belonging; you are worth it, whatever your "it" may be; and you have honored, loved, and nurtured your soul.

Imagine and know you are worthy of living happily and abundantly in harmony with yourself and others. Stay close to those things making you feel glad you are alive.

I Am Worth It Next Steps:

1. Tell two people you love how much joy and fulfillment they bring into your life. Do it this week, and continue to say it often.

2. You have the power to do something special for yourself. What will it be this week, and next week, and the week after that?

3. What will you add to your life this week and next week that will make you feel more fully alive?

4. What specific things will you do for two people in your life this week to help them feel more fully alive?

Based upon my observations and insights this week:

I will stop _____

_____.

I will start _____

_____.

I will continue _____

_____.

You bring great energy and joy to life and to others because of who you are. You are a blessing to many.

You ARE Worth It!

ACKNOWLEDGMENTS

It is with deep gratitude and appreciation that I acknowledge and thank the people in my life who have encouraged and supported me throughout this writing process in various different capacities, as well as in life. I have been truly blessed.

For Mark LeBlanc, my business coach, mentor, and friend who planted the seed to write this book…well, he actually gave it to me as a coaching assignment, which was non-negotiable. Thank you.

For Molly Harvey, my soul sister and colleague, who has encouraged me to write since we met at our first National Speakers Association (NSA) conference in 2001. Even though the Atlantic Ocean separates us physically, we have never been apart.

For my sisters Peggy Stokman and Anne Barden, for your love, support, encouragement and mentoring throughout my life.

For Mary Orfield, my long-time friend, for sharing your hospitality and beautiful home with me in Tucson where I began my writing using mind-maps, not having a concrete roadmap, trusting my intuition and the guidance I received. Our hikes, deep conversations, and beautiful scenery were an inspiration and blessing to me, as you are wherever we are.

For Natashia Halikowski, my soul sister from Calgary, whom I met at a NSA convention in 2002, for walking by my side, as you gave me continuous encouragement, feedback, and support over the years. Thank you for always sharing your beautiful, generous heart and wisdom.

For Georgine Madden, whose wisdom and generosity blesses me deeply, personally and professionally. I have learned much from you and appreciate the ways in which you invite me to grow.

For Karla Buckner, Katy Holden and Shelley Haiker, three great women, whose unwavering love and support of every aspect of my life, including the unfolding of this book, have enriched my life. We have been blessed to travel with each other through many life transitions.

For Pat Voss, Marilyn McGuire, and Jill Marks, long-time friends and colleagues, thank you for your precious friendship and support as well as taking time to read my manuscript, offering concrete suggestions to make it more clear and meaningful.

For Trish Storhoff, Nancy Roach, M.E.G. Roy, Theresa Pesch, and Kristin Ford Hinrichs, who supported and encouraged me throughout this process using the gifts you bring to the world. You remind me of how a quick "check-in" with someone can make a valuable contribution to that person's life, as it has for mine.

For Paul R. Scheele, Ph.D., for the transformational work that has occurred within me as a result of your creation and facilitation of the Ultimate You Retreat, Inner Circle, and monthly individual and group coaching. You are brilliant, wise and kind.

For Jill Strunk, Ph.D., for keeping me on track while offering valuable support in my healing process.

For Cheryl Leitschuh, Ed.D who helped me in the beginning stages of my manuscript and flow of topics. Your input gave me direction.

For Rita Webster, Ph.D., remembering our first and only writer's weekend away. It got us going, and was also fun.

For Deb Brown, my Monday morning accountability partner, for listening with a kind and discerning ear as we set goals, and then held each other accountable.

For Meg Hume, who continues to help me show up at my best so that I can forge ahead with confidence in the work I do.

For other family members, friends and clients as you have enriched my life, and taught me valuable lessons. You have contributed to the content of this 52-week process.

For Mark LeBlanc, Bob Danzig, Molly Harvey, Christine Clifford, Julie Gilbert Newrai, Deirdre Van Nest and Judy Kay Mausolf who took the time to write endorsements for my book. You are a blessing to me and to others. The work and gifts you bring to the world are phenomenal. We support each other.

Without the expertise of the following people, this book would not be published in its current form.

Thanks to:

Connie Anderson, Words & Deeds, Inc., for your brilliant editing skills.

Betty Liedtke, for your excellence as a proofreader.

Rena Lindgren, my computer assistant (angel) who makes sure everything works and happens.

Dara Beevas and her team's expert guidance during the publishing process at Wise Ink Creative Publishing.

It is my hope that you, the reader, will learn more about each of them, their expertise, the work that they do, the contributions they make in our world, including each person I have mentioned. You are all so worth it.

With deep gratitude,

Louise

ABOUT THE AUTHOR

Louise Griffith of One Shining Light, is an internationally recognized speaker, psychologist, and success coach who helps her clients get clear about what they want and then achieve it. She works with people who want to know what makes them tick and motivates them to take action in a positive and productive way. Her training deals with the core issues that stand in the way of performance and how people can be their best on a daily basis.

Under her spirited and practical guidance, people learn how to access their power, eliminate self-defeating behaviors, build on their strengths, and tap into their passion. Louise challenges her clients to explore how their thoughts impact their actions. The result? Better choices, improved communication, richer relationships, life-changing insights, and increased success. She lives in Minneapolis, Minnesota.

Speaking, Breakout Sessions, Coaching
To get on Louise's calendar, call (952) 484-3100
or email Louise at louise@oneshininglight.com
www.oneshininglight.com